A Practical Guide to Secondary Liability and Joint Enterprise Post-Jogee

A Practical Guide to Secondary Liability and Joint Enterprise Post-Jogee

Jo Cecil LLB (Hons) (Card)
Barrister

James Mehigan LLB (Hons) (Dubl),
MPhil (Cantab), PhD (Open), SFHEA
Barrister (England & Wales, Ireland, Northern Ireland)

Law Brief Publishing

Published 2020 by Law Brief Publishing, an imprint of Law Brief Publishing Ltd
30 The Parks
Minehead
Somerset
TA24 8BT

www.lawbriefpublishing.com

Paperback: 978-1-911035-41-1

PREFACE

It is now 4 years since the Supreme Court and Privy Council sat together for the first time to consider one of the most complicated and frustrating areas of criminal law. The law of joint enterprise had become muddled and, in our opinion, extremely unfair in the years since 1984 when the Privy Council had introduced the concept of foresight as a principle of law rather than a matter of evidence.

The case is by far the most significant criminal law case in the history of the UK Supreme Court and has radically altered the criminal law, with immediate effect for those accused of crimes in association with others. What it has not done is help those who have been convicted under the erroneous law in the years in which it was enforced. Some of these people received the death penalty in various jurisdictions, others received life sentences.

Now is an opportune time to take another look at the case and how it has been applied in practice. This book takes stock of the decision and its impact and looks at how it has been interpreted by the various agencies of the criminal justice system such at the Court of Appeal and the Crown Prosecution Service. It is only with the benefit of this long view that we can begin to understand the significance of the case.

We would like to thank many people who made this book possible and without whose support we would never be able to carry on our practices. These include our clerks and colleagues at Garden Court Chambers, and the colleagues with whom we worked in the Supreme Court and Privy Council, Mr Justice Julian Knowles, Matthew Blower, Deirdre Lyons-LeCroix, Peggy Morrison, Frances FitzGibbon QC, Caoilfhionn Gallagher QC, Daniella Waddoup, Shauneen Lambe and Jennifer Twite. We would also like to thank our publishers Tim Kevan and Garry Wright for their endless patience and assistance with putting this book together. Finally, we can't thank our families enough for putting up with us through the hours of hiding away writing this book that they had to put up with. We appreciate the support from every source.

We have tried to state the law as of 1 January 2020.

Jo Cecil
James Mehigan
Garden Court Chambers
January 2020

CONTENTS

INTRODUCTION

The criminal law is not very good at dealing with the murky cases where more than one person is accused of a crime. It is not well tooled to divide out the competing expectations of parties and even if it were the law is not very good at deciding what liability should attach and in what proportion to each party. That is why undergraduate criminal law students struggle so much with the doctrine of 'joint enterprise'. Indeed, the doctrine is so difficult that in 1984 a senior judge from New Zealand got the law wrong while sitting in judgment of a case from Hong Kong, in a courtroom in London. His one paragraph summation of the law, backed up with no authority, provided a useful tool for prosecutors and became adopted by many jurisdictions. The House of Lords went so far as to double down on the principle that it is enough to have foresight of a co-defendant's actions to be liable for them, even if you do not intend them.

The 'foresight principle' has clearly had a deleterious effect on the lives of many people who served lengthy sentences and in some cases were executed having been convicted on the basis of this erroneous law. It was not until 2016 that the Supreme Court, in a legal first, sat in a conjoined hearing with the Privy Council to hear a case from England and a case from Jamaica, with a view to correcting this longstanding legal error.

This book attempts to explain how we got here and consider what we are to do to make sense of it. For, although the Supreme Court and Privy Council corrected the erroneous law, this has not given much succour to the many who were wrongfully convicted. The first chapter looks at the legal history of the principle of 'joint enterprise' and how it lead to the historic case of *R v Jogee; Ruddock v The Queen*[1] (which will be referred to as *Jogee* throughout the volume).

1 [2016] UKSC 8; [2016] UKPC 7.

The decision in *Jogee* is one which appears to have cleared up the law going forward. As discussed in the final chapter, it has altered charging procedures and this appears to have had an impact on the management of cases and sentencing outcomes. In one sense, this is the easy bit. Judges apply the law in good faith and the outcome of a well-reasoned Supreme Court judgment will be felt throughout the justice system. What is much more problematic is that trial judges had been applying the erroneous law in good faith for over a quarter of a century. What is to be done about the hundreds of people convicted of crimes, including murders, that they did not commit.

Chapter 3 begins with a pragmatic approach. It discusses how the historic appeal can be approach to give the applicant the best chance of success before the Court of Appeal. However, the outlook is not a good one. As Chapters 4 & 5 demonstrate, the number of successful appeals is vanishingly small. At the time of going to press, only two appeals had succeeded. These are discussed in detail in Chapter 4 so the reader can join us in trying to discern why these cases were successful. This is no easy task because it can be hard to see the difference between these cases and the unsuccessful cases considered in Chapter 5. We have tried to draw out some threads of consistency to gain an understanding of the Court's doctrinal position on the historic appeals that arise out of *Jogee*. Though it appears that the case law demonstrates a loose pragmatism rather than a clearly thought out process for dealing with such cases.

The legal framework now in place means that it is exceptionally difficult to appeal against a conviction which is founded on an incorrect interpretation of the law. We hope that this volume will help explain how that has come to be the case and perhaps help those navigating these difficult cases to be successful in their applications.

CHAPTER ONE
JOINT ENTERPRISE BEFORE JOGEE

The term 'joint enterprise' is an imprecise, broad and often misunderstood piece of legal terminology. In February 2016 the Supreme Court and the Judicial Committee of the Privy Council sat together for the first time and stated that since 1984 one aspect of the principle of joint enterprise had been wrongly applied since 1984.

This book will discuss the history of the principle of joint enterprise as well as the decision in Jogee itself and how that has had an impact on the application of law. Then go on to discuss what this means for those who have been convicted under the law as it stood between 1984 and 2016 and what it means for those who stand accused of offences involving multiple defendants in the future.

What is joint enterprise?

The term 'joint enterprise' appears on the face of it to be a legal term understood by lawyers and used by criminal justice practitioners to clearly describe a particular phenomenon. The truth is that it is far less precise than that. 'Joint enterprise' is a label that papers over a confusing aspect of the criminal law. It is not built on solid, clear legal foundations and it covers such a broad set of circumstances that it is difficult to think of its use as adding clarity to the understanding of the criminal law. Jogee has gone some way to clearing up this confusion, but before we discuss the case itself it is important to unpick what is included in joint enterprise.

'Joint enterprise' can largely be considered to comprise three components; joint principals, accessories and instances where more than one person is involved in a crime and someone within that groups goes further to commit another crime. It is worth considering each of these in turn.

The liability of joint principals is an easy one to understand both conceptually and morally. If two or more people commit a crime, each is guilty of the offence. If two people attack another, they are both guilty of assault. Similarly, if two people go into a corner shop with the intention of threatening the sales assistant, they are both guilty of the offence of robbery. Both offenders share the common purpose of the offence and thus this is often known as **common purpose liability**.

This appears to be the best (or at least simplest) use of the term 'joint enterprise' in the sense that both offenders have decided to engage in a criminal 'enterprise' together. The language of business administration has crept into the criminal law for this doctrine, implying that both parties are engaging in an agreed plan of risk taking activity with a view to making a profit from it, or at least benefiting from it in some way.

One step removed from this simple form of joint enterprise is the role of the accessory. This is also known as 'aiding and abetting' and under section 8 of the Accessories and Abettors Act 1861 accessory 'shall be liable to be tried, indicted and punished as a principal offender'. This applies to anybody who encouraged or helped the principal offender to commit the offence even if they are not present when the offence committed. The classic example is the getaway driver but one can also think of many other accessories such as somebody who provides or hides a weapon or who attends offence with a view to providing strength in numbers. In each of these cases the accessory intends the offence to occur and provide some form of assistance or encouragement. This '**basic accessorial liability**' is also a form of 'joint enterprise' as all the parties are engaged in the same enterprise, however it is not this form of joint enterprise with which *Jogee* is concerned.

The prosecution of joint principals and basic accessories is a relatively straightforward exercise. It is not this particular type of prosecution which has caused the significant controversy and confusion. That arises from the doctrine of '**parasitic accessorial liability**' ('PAL'). The name[1] is something of a mouthful because it deals with a very particular set of circumstances. That set of circumstances where two or more people form the common intention to commit a crime and arising from that crime a second crime is committed by one of the parties. One of the other parties can be found guilty if he had *foresight* that this offence might occur.

The Supreme Court in the case of *Gnango* describes it in these terms: 'Parasitic accessory liability arises where (i) D1 and D2 have a common intention to commit crime A (ii) D1, as an incident of committing crime A, commits crime B, and (iii) D2 had foreseen the possibility that he might do so.'[2] This is a technical way to describe the occurrence in almost algebraic terms, but breaking down the name of this form of liability may help explain just how particular it is. It is a form of accessorial liability because it allows for somebody who did not commit the direct *actus reus* of the offence to be found guilty of it by way of secondary involvement. It is 'parasitic' because it relates to a second crime which arises in the course of conduct for the first crime. This liability for the second crime is considered to be 'parasitic' because it is dependent on the first crime. The accessory cannot be found guilty of the second crime if he has not been involved in the first crime in some way.

Before the decision in Jogee, the law had settled on the principle that if you were involved in the first crime and you could foresee the possibility of a second crime being committed by one of your party then you were also guilty of that second crime. Jogee has now made clear that this was an incorrect interpretation of the law. To understand the significance of the Jogee case it is worth considering the history and context of the doctrine of parasitic accessorial liability.

---

1 The name was coined by Professor John Smith, Smith, J (1997) 'Criminal liability of accessories: law and law reform', *Law Quarterly Review*, 113 (Jul), 453-467, at p 455.

2 *Gnango* [2012] 1 AC 827, para 42.

History and context of the decision in Jogee

It is possible to take a historical view of the doctrine of joint enterprise that looks back over many centuries. Indeed after the Supreme Court gave its decision in Jogee the then chairman of the Criminal Bar Association[3] described the legal submissions by the appellants as a 'feat of forensic archaeology, digging through the layers of decisions over five centuries, to reveal the origins and development of the law of secondary liability, whereby those indirectly involved in crime can be found guilty along with the principal offenders.'[4] The cases date back as far as a murder case in 1556 and include the prosecution of those involved in duelling, apple thieves killing watchmen and gamekeepers being shot by poachers. For the purposes of this book a somewhat shorter discussion of the history is useful[5].

Until the late Twentieth Century the criminal law relied upon either common purpose liability for basic accessorial liability. As one retired Court of Appeal judge put it, 'Until 1983 the law of secondary liability, although unsatisfactory in many ways, was fairly clear'[6]. The law before 1983 required intention. As Baker puts it 'the Australian precedents, as well as the English precedents going back 500 years, support interpreting complicitiy as requiring nothing less than intention. The Supreme Court of the United States also has held that the ancient

3 Francis FitzGibbon QC acted on behalf of one of the interveners in the case, Just for Kids Law.

4 FitzGibbon, F (2016) 'Joint Enterprise', *London Review of Books*, Vol 38, No 5, p 26.

5 For a fuller treatment of the historical context see Knowles, J (2016), 'Joint Enterprise After *Jogee and Ruddock*: What Next?', *UK Supreme Court Yearbook,* Vol 7, pp 72-128.

6 Buxton, R (2016), 'Jogee: upheaval in secondary liability for murder', *Crim LR*, Vol 5, pp 324-333.

English authorities support interpreting the mental element in complicity as requiring nothing less than intention[7]'.[8]

Although a step was made in the direction of PAL in the 19th Century case of *Macklin* which allowed for the secondary offender to be found guilty of murder if they 'both must have realised that resistance at all costs was likely'[9].

In the course of the 1960s & 1970s cases reaffirmed that intent was necessary for the parasitic crime. In the 1963 case of *Wesley Smith*[10] the trial judge's summing up that '[o]nly he who intended that unlawful and grievous bodily harm should be done is guilty of murder. He who intended that the victim should be unlawfully hit and hurt will be guilty of manslaughter if death results.'[11] The Court of Criminal Appeal described this jury direction as 'legally unassailable'[12]. This is a clear statement that it is intention and no less that was considered to be required and the summing up was approved by Lord Parker CJ in *Betty*[13].

A fatal stabbing lead to the conviction of one defendant for murder and one for manslaughter in the case of *Anderson and Morris*[14]. The evidence against Morris for the manslaughter was 'unclear' and the judge directed the jury that if there was a common design to attack the victim and Anderson took out a knife, which Morris did not know of, and

7 *Rosemond v US* (2014) 134 S Ct 1240.

8 Baker, D (2017), 'Letter to the editor: *Jogee*: jury directions and the manslaughter alternative', Crim LR 51-56, p51. See also Baker, D (2016), *Reinterpreting Complicity and Inchoate Participation Offences*, London: Routledge.

9 [1831] 4 Car & P 565.

10 [1963] 1 WLR 1200.

11 [1963] 1 WLR 1200 at 1206 and *Jogee* [28].

12 [1963] 1 WLR 1200 at 1207.

13 [1964] 48 Cr App R 6 and *Jogee* [30].

14 [1966] 2 QB 110.

used that weapon to kill, then Morris is liable only for manslaughter. The five judge Court of Criminal Appeal heard submissions, which were accepted, that the authorities from approximately 1830 onwards established the principal that the second defendant is not liable for events which go 'beyond what has been tacitly agreed'[15].

The Court in Anderson and Morris was not resiling itself from the decisions in *Wesley Smith* and *Betty*, (where someone joins a multi-handed criminal endeavour, he will not be guilty of murder if there is an escalation of that endeavour, unless he has the mens rea for murder). It was saying that an 'overwhelming supervening event' may be the actual cause of the death, rather than a mere escalation of a fight[16].

This position was confirmed in the case of *Reid*[17] in 1976. In that case 3 alleged supporters of the Irish Republican Army went to the house of a British colonel. One of their number shot him dead and two of them were convicted of murder, while the Appellant was convicted of manslaughter. He unsuccessfully appealed on the basis that there was no evidence for finding that he had intention to cause any harm. The jury had rejected this defence and their verdict meant that he must have intended some, at least minimal, harm be caused by his actions. The Court stated that in such cases: 'If such injury was not intended by the others they must be acquitted of murder; but having started out on an enterprise which envisaged some degree of violence, albeit nothing more than causing fright, they will be guilty of manslaughter'.[18]

The Privy Council decision in *Chan Wing Siu*

At the start of 1984 the law in complicity cases, as noted above, was fairly settled. It may not have been perfect, but it was clear. Intention was at the heart of liability for such cases. However in June of that year,

15 [1966] 2 QB 110 at 118 and *Jogee* [31]

16 *Jogee* [33].

17 [1976] 62 Cr App R 109.

18 [1976] 62 Cr App R 109 and *Jogee* [35].

in a case from Hong Kong, the Judicial Committee of the Privy Council (the 'Privy Council') handed down a judgment which was to substantially change that. At its simplest, that case, *Chan Wing-Siu*[19] reduced the mental element for secondary liability to *foresight* of possibility of the parasitic crime rather than *intention* that it be committed. It is this change that the appellants in *Jogee* & *Ruddock* submitted was where the law had 'jumped the tracks'. This reduction of the mental element was incorrect in its interpretation of the common law as it stood at the time and it marked the effective birth of parasitic accessorial liability. The Supreme Court in *Jogee* agreed, but before we come to the reasoning for that decision it remains important to discuss *Chan Wing Siu* and the major authorities that derived from it, particularly *Powell and Daniels*[20] which solidified the principle in the law of England and Wales.

The facts in *Chan Wing-Siu* are not attractive. Three men entered a prostitute's home armed with knives. They intended to rob her husband but in the end they killed him and she was slashed on the head with a knife. All three were convicted of murder and wounding with intent to cause grievous bodily harm. The appeal was run on the basis that if the conditions for using a knife occurred (for example, resistance by the victim) then the prosecution must prove that the defendant foresaw a likelihood of greater than 50% that one of his co-accused would act with intent to cause death or really serious harm. This contrived ground of appeal was rejected. As the Court in *Jogee* describe it; 'There was an overwhelming case for inferring that the appellants foresaw the likelihood of resistance and that their plan included the possible use of knives to cause serious harm.'[21]

The Privy Council did not need to do much by way of considered jurisprudence to dismiss the appeal. It would simply have been enough to reason that the evidence in the case was so strong that there was

19 [1985] 1 AC 168.

20 [1999] 1 AC 1.

21 *Jogee* at [36-37].

intention to use violence in the case of resistance.[22] The facts could easily be read as evidence of common purpose liability. However the judgment of the Court went beyond this and upheld the convictions on a different basis. It is worth repeating the passage from *Chan Wing-Siu* cited by the Court in *Jogee* here.

> *In the typical case [of aiding and abetting] the same or the same type of offence is actually intended by all the parties acting in concert. In view of the terms of the directions to the jury here, the Crown does not seek to support the present convictions on that ground. The case must depend rather on the wider principle whereby a secondary party is criminally liable for acts by the primary offender of a type which the former foresees but does not necessarily intend.*
>
> *That there is such a principle is not in doubt. It turns on contemplation or, putting the same idea in other words, authorisation, which may be express but is more usually implied. It meets the case of a crime foreseen as a possible incident of the common unlawful enterprise. The criminal liability lies in participating in the venture with that foresight.*[23]

As discussed above, this is not consistent with the preceding 500 years of case law and is unnecessary on the facts for the purposes of dismissing the appeal. In effect it amounted to a major shift in the law of complicity. The Court in *Jogee* is highly critical of the methods by which this conclusion was reached. While *Anderson and Morris* is cited, none of the case law dating back to 1830 is not made reference to. It will also not have escaped the reader's eye that Sir Robin Cooke makes the sweeping statement about there being 'no doubt' that such a principle (of secondary liability based on foresight) exists, but does not provide evidence to support it from the English law.

---

22 *Jogee* at [37]

23 *Chan Wing-Siu*, p175.

The effective outcome of the judgment was to turn a long-standing rule of evidence into a rule of law. From this point on foresight was no longer a useful way to assess if the required intention was there, foresight was now the intention itself. This was the moment, it was submitted on behalf of Ruddock, when the law 'jumped the tracks'. This was a submission that was accepted by the Court. The law was wrongly interpreted in the Privy Council and it was compounded by later decisions there and in the House of Lords.

In *Hui Chi Ming*[24] the Privy Council considered another murder appeal from Hong Kong. In this case the application of the principle in *Chan Wing-Siu* lead to the secondary offender (the appellant) being convicted of murder when the principal offender was only convicted of manslaughter. A group of six young men went in search of a man who had allegedly intimidated one of their girlfriends. They began a search for 'someone to hit' and the principal, whose girlfriend had been the subject of the intimidation, was armed with a length of pipe. An innocent man who met the description of the intimidator was chanced upon and the principal attacked him with the pipe. The principal was charged with murder but found guilty only of manslaughter [25]. The appellant was later arrested and charged with murder as he had engaged in a joint enterprise in which the principal had committed murder. The jury was directed that entering a joint enterprise in which a co-entrepreneur had a weapon which could be used to apply lethal force and the weapon was so used then liability for murder would attach. The jury was not directed that the principal who struck the blow must have at least contemplated serious harm would result from the blow. Unaware that the principal had been acquitted of murder (as this was not admitted, in spite of defence submissions) the jury found the appellant guilty of murder and he was sentenced to death. With regard to PAL the Privy Council stated:

---

24 *Hui Chi Ming* [1992] 1 AC 34.

25 Two other members of the group pleaded guilty to manslaughter and one was acquitted after judicial direction.

> *The defendant's second point relies on Sir Robin Cooke's use of the word 'authorisation' as a synonym for contemplation in the passage already cited from his judgment in Chan Wing-Siu v. The Queen [1985] A.C. 168, 175. Their Lordships consider that Sir Robin used this word – and in that regard they do not differ from counsel – to emphasise the fact that mere foresight is not enough: the accessory, in order to be guilty, must have foreseen the relevant offence which the principal may commit as a possible incident of the common unlawful enterprise and must, with such foresight, still have participated in the enterprise. The word 'authorisation' explains what is meant by contemplation, but does not add a new ingredient. That this is so is manifest from Sir Robin's pithy conclusion to the passage cited: 'The criminal culpability lies in participating in the venture with that foresight.'*[26]

The effect of this judgment then is to take the actual intention of the principal out of the foresight test for PAL. You can be found guilty of the offence if you contemplated that a murder would be committed, even if a murder was not actually committed by the principal. The case had the effect of developing and confirming the doctrine of PAL as established in *Chan Wing-Siu*, but it was not until 1996 that the House of Lords considered it.

Prior to the case of *Powell and Daniels*[27] the principles set out in Chan Wing Siu were steadily adopted as a principle of English law by the Court of Appeal in a series of cases[28]. However, it was not until it reached the House of Lords in the conjoined appeals of *Powell and Daniels* and *English*[29] that the mistake of law at the heart of PAL was finally ossified into the criminal law of England & Wales.

---

26 Per Lord Lowry, [1992] 1 A.C. 34, at p 53.

27 *Powell and Daniels; English* [1999] 1 A.C. 1; [1997] 3 W.L.R. 959; [1998] 1 Cr. App. R. 261.

28 Their Lordships in Jogee [at paras 47-50] provide the examples of *Slack* [1989] QB 775, *Wakely* [1990] Crim LR 119 and *Hyde* [1991] 1 QB 134.

29 The case is referred to as *Powell and Daniels* for brevity in this book.

The case essentially confirms the position in *Chan Wing-Siu* by stating that foresight is sufficient for liability in such cases. Lord Steyn stated that '[f]oresight and intention are not synonymous terms. But foresight is a necessary and sufficient ground of the liability of accessories'[30]. Essentially their Lordships determined that it was sufficient for secondary liability to attach if the accomplice thought that the principal might kill with intent even when the accomplice did not hold such an intention himself. This reasoning lead to two disturbing facets of secondary liability. The first is the possibility that a secondary party can be found guilty of a murder when neither they nor the principal had intended serious harm or death from their actions. The second was the creation of the defence of 'fundamental difference'.

Lord Hutton explicitly addressed the fact that there can be illogical outcomes from common law rules. 'In my opinion there are practical considerations of weight and importance related to considerations of public policy which justify the principle stated in *Chan Wing-Siu* and which prevail over considerations of strict logic.'[31] In effect their Lordships were admitting that there would be some phenomenally unjust outcomes (remember that the appellant in *Hui Chi-Ming* was facing the death penalty) but this was overridden by public policy concerns. The public policy concern is usually framed in terms of creating an effective deterrent to those who engage in violence as part of a group. What that effectively comes down to is ensuring more people are convicted by making life easier for the prosecution. For 500 years prosecutors had to prove intention but between *Chan Wing-Siu* and *Powell and Daniels* that changed into a requirement that they prove mere foresight. The law's wrong turning in *Chan Wing-Siu* was (almost) indelibly etched on the criminal law to make life easier for the prosecution.

While Powell and Daniels solidified PAL it also developed it. In response to some of the manifest unfairness of the doctrine their Lordships created the 'fundamental difference' rule. This was the only let out

30 *Powell and Daniels* [1999] 1 A.C. 1, at p 13.

31 *Powell and Daniels* [1999] 1 A.C. 1, at p 23.

valve from the illogical outcomes that would inevitably follow from a strictly applied foresight rule. The fundamental difference rule, as Knowles demonstrates[32], arose from the difficult facts of the appeal of *English* (conjoined to *Powell and Daniels*). In English the principal and secondary offender attacked a police officer with wooden poles. After the secondary had fled, the principal stabbed the officer with a knife that the secondary did not know about. Under the principle in Chan Wing-Siu, logically applied, liability would attach to a secondary offender who engaged in an attack with one type of weapon but whose co-attacker, unbeknownst to the secondary, was carrying a weapon of a different order of lethality[33].

While the legal effect of *Powell & Daniels* was to settle the principle in *Chan Wing-Siu* as the basis for liability in PAL cases in England & Wales, it is hard to overemphasise the deleterious impact this settled law has had on the criminal justice system in general and the right to a fair trial in particular. The so-called 'public policy reasons' for expanding liability for parasitic offences has allowed for a broadly applied principle to assist prosecutors in convicting those only peripherally involved in an offence. In effect, this reduces the work required by the prosecutor to prove involvement in an offence because, as a former client of ours once said, it is a 'lazy law'. It has had a particularly damaging effect on young black men[34].

The PAL principle should apply to all cases where a parasitic 'crime B' occurs (for example one party assaulting a security guard when two people are shoplifting). However, its most damaging effects are particularly problematic in cases of murder. This is to do with the fact that a murder conviction carries with it the highest level of stigma conceived of by the criminal law and also a mandatory life sentence. At the time of

---

32 Knowles, op cit, pp 110-111.

33 *Powell and Daniels* [1999] 1 A.C. 1, per Lord Hutton at p 28.

34 Phillips, C & Bowling, B (2017), 'Ethnicities, racism, crime and criminal justice', in Liebling, A, Maruna, S & McAra, L (eds), *Oxford Handbook of Criminology* (6th ed), Oxford: Oxford University Press, pp 190-212.

Chan Wing-Siu and Powell and Daniels were decided the decision on how long a prisoner must stay in custody before being eligible to apply for parole (their minimum term) was determined by the Home Secretary. In a House of Lords judgment in 2002 this political process was found to be incompatible with the Human Rights Act 1998[35]. In response to this removal of his powers the then Home Secretary, David Blunkett, introduced in section 269 of the Criminal Justice Act 2003 a strict system for determining the minimum term to be served in murder cases[36]. This largely tied the hands of judges. Notably, by including offending in groups as an aggravating factor, it created a situation where many defendants receiving long sentences even though they were only liable for murder because they had a minimum level of foresight but limited meaningful involvement in the offence. It is quite possible within the guidance to imagine someone actually stabbing someone in cold blood receiving a significantly shorter sentence than someone who attended a fight that ended in a death.

Their hands tied by the guidelines, judges have been imposing condign sentences with a real disconnect from the gravity of the offending.

The decision in Jogee & Ruddock

It is in this context that the Supreme Court and Privy Council came to hear these conjoined cases. These courts[37] had never heard cases together in the past and on that fact alone the case was a historical development. The reasons for the joinder appear to stem from the fact that the mistake of law was made in a Privy Council case (*Chan Wing-Siu*) and ossified in England and Wales by the House of Lords (*Powell*

35 *R (on the application of Anderson) v Secretary of State for the Home* Department [2002] UKHL 46; [2003] 1 AC 87; [2003] 1 Cr App R 32.

36 Crewe, B, A Liebling, N Padfield & G Virgo (2015) 'Joint enterprise: the implications of an unfair and unclear law', *Crim LR*, Vol 4, 252-269.

37 Nor indeed had the Supreme Court's predecessor, the Judicial Committee of the House of Lords, considered a case with the Privy Council.

and Daniels). To unambiguously correct this their Lordships appear to have taken the view that it needed a unified decision of both courts.

It is useful to have a brief summary of the factual and appellate history of the two cases here. Mr Jogee was convicted of murder having gone with the principal to the house of the victim which the principal entered uninvited. They had been to the house a number of times that night and on the final occasion the principal entered the victim's kitchen and stabbed him with a knife he found there. Mr Jogee remained outside when this happened. He was smashing a bottle against a car and shouting encouragement. Both men were convicted on 28 March 2012. The facts of the case are such that it, like so many of the cases upon which PAL is built[38], is not actually a PAL case. The murder is not a parasitic 'crime B' that derives from a 'crime A' which the parties initially embarked on.

Mr Jogee appealed his conviction to the Court of Appeal[39] and, perhaps unsurprisingly in the light of *Powell and Daniels*, the trial judge's directions on joint enterprise were found to be satisfactory. He appealed this decision to the Supreme Court and it is this appeal that was heard by the Court of five members alongside that of Mr Ruddock.

Mr Ruddock was a fish merchant in Jamaica who was arrested alongside the principal and a third person in a car which belonged to the deceased. The deceased had been missing for some days. The principal pleaded guilty to murder. The case against Mr Ruddock at trial was pleaded in two alternatives. Either he and the principal entered into an agreement to rob and kill the victim or they entered an agreement to rob him and Mr Ruddock must have foreseen that the principal might have stabbed him with at least the intention of serious harm. Mr Ruddock's defence was that he had not been present at the murder and had no knowledge of it. He explained his incriminating statements to

38 For example *Chan Wing-Siu* was factually not a case which required PAL in order to found liability.

39 *Jogee* [2013] EWCA Crim 1433

an investigating officer as the result of beatings he received. These facts are a much better example of a case involving PAL than those in *Jogee*. If the jury found that Mr Ruddock was party to a plan to rob and kill, then PAL is not required, common purpose liability is sufficient. However, if they found that he had only entered a plan to rob the victim PAL is required for the prosecution to found liability. This is perhaps a perfect example of PAL acting as a catch all safety net for a prosecution founded on very weak evidence. When a prosecution can't prove intention, as was impossible in Mr Ruddock's case, PAL can be relied upon to found liability for murder in the absence of intention. However, this safety net was quite poorly constructed even on its own terms. During oral argument, counsel for the DPP of Jamaica conceded that the trial judge's direction on joint enterprise was not a good example of a proper *Chan Wing-Siu* direction in any event.

The judgment in *Jogee* marks a major change in the law on joint enterprise, so it is worth considering the way the Supreme Court and Privy Council have set this out. The judgment sets out the new test early but then goes on to a detailed historical analysis of the law on secondary liability.

The correct test for parasitic accessorial liability is one of intention, not of foresight and this means that the 1984 case, notwithstanding how often it has been faithfully applied at trial, cannot stand. At paragraph 79 the Court sets out its succinct conclusion on the *Chan Wing-Siu* decision:

> *It will be apparent from what we have said that we do not consider that the Chan Wing-Siu principle can be supported, except on the basis that it has been decided and followed at the highest level. In plain terms, our analysis leads us to the conclusion that the introduction of the principle was based on an incomplete, and in some respects erroneous, reading of the previous case law, coupled with generalised and questionable policy arguments.*

The judgment gives five reasons why it is right to reverse the decision in *Chan Wing-Siu*. These are worth setting out as they give a clear indication of the Court's reasoning and also an explanation of how it felt it had the power to make such significant changes. In essence these reasons are that:

1. The Court in *Jogee* has had the benefit of a 'much fuller analysis than on previous occasions when the topic has been considered'. They note that only two English cases are cited in *Chan Wing-Siu* itself and while more were referred to in *Powell and Daniels; English*, many important cases were missed out.[40]

2. The current law on PAL, based on *Chan Wing-Siu* is not working satisfactorily. It needs to be corrected because it 'remains highly controversial and a continuing source of difficulty for trial judges. It ahs also led to large numbers of appeals.'[41]

3. Secondary liability 'is an important part of the common law, and if a wrong turn has been taken, it should be corrected.[42] The Court rejected the argument that the passage of time means that Parliament should make any amendments to the doctrine. Because it is a common law doctrine that has been 'unduly widened by the courts, it is proper for the courts to correct the error'.[43]

4. The role of foresight has been greatly overvalued in the post *Chan Wing-Siu* jurisprudence. At common law foresight was no more than evidence from which the jury could work whether the defendant had the necessary intention. The Court in Jodie noted that murder already has a relatively low mens rea

40 *Jogee* at paragraph 80.

41 *Jogee* at paragraph 81.

42 *Jogee* at paragraph 82.

43 *Jogee* at paragraph 85.

threshold because liability attaches once the defendant intended to cause really serious harm even if they did not intend to kill.

The *Chan Wing-Siu* principle extends liability for murder to a secondary party on the basis of a still lesser degree of culpability, namely foresight only of the possibility of the principle may commit murder but without there being any need for the intention to assist them to do so. It savours, as Prof Smith suggested, of constructed crime.[44]

5. The fifth point that the Court made is that the rule creates the 'striking anomaly' whereby a secondary offender can be found guilty on the basis of a lower threshold than the principal offender.

For these reasons the Court determined that it was able to reverse the principle in *Chan Wing-Siu* and return to the law as it stood for centuries prior to that decision.

Early on in the judgment the true test for secondary liability in PAL cases is set out. After all the confusion that has developed with the interpretation of Chan Wing-Siu the test is for secondary liability generally as set out in *Jogee* is a simple one: 'The requisite conduct element is that D2 has encouraged or assisted the commission of the offence by D1.'[45] In PAL cases specifically the Court goes on to say 'the mental element in assisting or encouraging to assist or encourage the commission of the crime and this requires knowledge of any existing facts necessary for it to be criminal'[46]. This means that if 'the crime requires a particular intent, D2 must intend to assist or encourage D1 to act with such intent'[47]. In those three paragraphs the Court has re-established the

44 *Jogee* at paragraph 83.

45 *Jogee* at paragraph 8.

46 *Jogee* at paragraph 9.

47 *Jogee* at paragraph 10.

principle of intention as an essential part of mens rea in PAL cases. The Judges then went on to set out more detail on the conduct and mental element required in such cases.

The conduct element or **actus reus** will involve an act of assistance or encouragement and the Court is clear that the potential way in which this will work will be highly fact specific. Association between D1 and D2 'may or may not involve assistance or encouragement' and the same is true for presence at the scene of a crime. 'Both association and presence are likely to be very relevant evidence on the question of whether assistance or encouragement was provided.'[48] It is noted that presence can amount to encouragement and can assist in the commission of violent crimes, even if no violence is perpetrated by the merely present D2. Once this assistance or encouragement is established, the prosecution does not have to prove that it ha a positive effect on D1's conduct. That means there is no 'but for' test. It will not be enough to say 'he would have done it anyway, it didn't matter that I was there is support'[49].

When it comes to the mental element or **mens rea** the Court was clear that the way in which intention to assist or encourage operates will be specific to particular offences. However, the D2 may intend to assist or encourage a particular category of offence without necessarily knowing which precise offence would be committed. A D2 could assist or encourage an offence of terrorism, without knowing the exact form it would take[50]. It is enough that they knew of a range of possible offences which they were assisting or encouraging.

So where does this leave **foresight**? The short answer is that it returns to its role as evidence of intention rather than as proof of common purpose. This latter use of foresight as proof positive that there was a

---

48 *Jogee* at paragraph 11.

49 *Jogee* at paragraph 12.

50 *Jogee* at paragraph 14.

common purpose (and therefore liability) was erroneous. The Court sets it out as follows:

> *The error was to equate foresight with intent to assist, as a matter of law; the correct approach is to treat it as evidence of intent. The long-standing pre-Chan Wing-Siu practice of inferring intent to assist from a common criminal purpose which includes the further crime, if the occasion for it were to arise, was always a legitimate one; what was illegitimate was to treat foresight as an inevitable yardstick of common purpose.*[51]

For practitioners in the future this has real significance. The defendant's knowledge that his associate might do something, however unlikely, is no longer enough for secondary liability. They must have intended it to happen and assist or encourage it. This will mean that prosecutors will now need evidence to prove someone's liability and will not be able to fall back neatly on the *Chan Wing-Siu* foresight safety net. This is a significant change and was felt immediately in the criminal courts.

The judgment's effect is to clarify the law and create a clearer and more logical basis upon which to found secondary liability in PAL cases. However, it does not mean that someone who lacks intent for a murder arising out of a violent 'crime A' will be without any criminal liability. If they engage in a violent offence which ends in death they can still be found guilty of **manslaughter**, notwithstanding the fact that they did not intend to cause really serious harm or death.[52] This may in certain cases appear to be particularly harsh but it has the benefit of taking a large number of cases out of the purview of the strict sentencing rules for murder. Murder convictions incur a mandatory life sentence and the fact that an offence was committed by a group (which will inevitably apply to almost all PAL murder convictions) serves to aggravate the component of the sentence which deals with the minimum term. The

---

51 *Jogee* at paragraph 87.

52 *Jogee* at paragraph 96. See also Ormerod, D & K Laird (2016) 'Jogee: Not the end of a legal saga but the start of one?', *Crim LR*, Vol 8, 539-552, at 543.

sentencing range for manslaughter on the other hand is broader than for almost any other offence ranging from a conditional discharge to a life sentence, although the trend in recent years has been towards sentences of immediate custody. The sentencing judge therefore has the ability to impose a sentence which fits the role played by the secondary offender in a much more precise fashion than was possible in the pre-*Jogee* legal framework.

The effect of the decision in Jogee is clear for those who are involved in PAL cases in the future, but the Court went on to discuss how appellate courts should deal with cases where juries were directed in good faith on the basis of Chan Wing-Siu. Before discussing those cases it may be of interest to readers to know the eventual outcome for the two appellants in this case, Jogee and Ruddock.

Mr Jogee's conviction was quashed and a re-trial was ordered. This took place in Nottingham Crown Court and resulted in Mr Jogee's conviction for manslaughter. He was sentenced to a 12-year determinate sentence.[53]

In the Privy Council it was accepted by counsel for the DPP of Jamaica that the appeal must be allowed if the principle in Chan Wing-Siu is wrong in law.[54] Mr Ruddock's case was remitted to the Court of Appeal of Jamaica. There it was decided that his quashed conviction for murder be substituted with a conviction for manslaughter. A new sentence of 17 years was imposed.[55]

For the two appellants in these cases then, the impact of the decision in *Jogee* is one with a significant impact on their sentence. However, for

---

53 Bowcott, O [2016] 'Ameen Jogee jailed for manslaughter in joint enterprise test case', *Guardian*, 12 September, available at <https://www.theguardian.com/law/2016/sep/12/ameen-jogee-jailed-manslaughter-police-officer-joint-enterprise-test-case>.

54 *Jogee* at paragraph 120.

55 *Shirley Ruddock v R* [2017] JMCA Crim 6.

those who were convicted prior to this decision the Supreme Court and Court of Appeal have contrived to ensure that there is likely to be little change. The mechanism by which this has taken place, and the means by which practitioners can hope to work with the legal framework, are the subject of the following chapters.

CHAPTER TWO JOHNSON AND SUBSTANTIAL INJUSTICE

As discussed, the Supreme Court in *Jogee* held that the common law had taken a 'wrong turn' in the 1985 case of *Chan Wing-Siu*. The Supreme Court's decision to quash the convictions for murder on this basis derives from the '*declaratory principle of the common law*'.[1]

Impact of Common Law Developments and Test to be Applied

The impact of a change in the common law post-conviction, as in *Jogee*, and the approach to be taken is perhaps most clearly expressed in the judgment of Lord Bingham in *Derek Bentley*:[2]

> *Where, between conviction and appeal, there have been significant changes in the common law (as opposed to changes effected by statute) or in standards of fairness, the approach indicated requires the Court to apply legal rules and procedural criteria which were not and could not reasonably have been applied at the time. This could cause difficulty in some cases but not, we conclude, in this.*

This arises from the statutory duty of the Court of Appeal to determine whether the conviction is safe. In short, where a case is concerned with common law developments, the Court applies the law as clarified and declared to be since the conviction when assessing the safety test.

---

1 Beevor, A (2013), 'The Declaratory Theory of Law', *Oxford Journal of Legal Studies*, Vol. 33(3), pp 421–444.

2 [2001] 1 Cr App R 21.

Bentley, a notorious case, concerned a conviction dating to 1952, which had been referred to the Court of Appeal by the CCRC in 1997. Applying the principles to the case, the Court considered:

> *(1) We must apply the substantive law of murder as applicable at the time, disregarding the abolition of constructive malice and the introduction of the defence of diminished responsibility by the Homicide Act 1957.*
>
> *(2) The liability of a party to a joint enterprise must be determined according to the common law as now understood.*
>
> *(3) The conduct of the trial and the direction of the jury must be judged according to the standards which we would now apply in any other appeal under section 1 of the 1968 Act.*
>
> *(4) We must judge the safety of the conviction according to the standards which we would now apply in any other appeal under section 1 of the 1968 Act.*

This however only applies to those cases which are actually before the Court and have been granted leave.

It is plain that the Supreme Court harboured considerable concerns in relation to opening the floodgates for potential appeals. As such, additional hurdles were put in place with regard to historic applications and out of time applications for leave to appeal against conviction. These have subsequently been said to meet '*the wider public interest in legal certainty and the finality of decisions made in accordance with the then clearly established law*'.[3]

---

3 *Johnson, Garwood, Green and others* [2017] 4 WLR 104 at para. 18

Out of Time Applications for Leave and Historic Appeals

Paragraph 100 of *Jogee* considered the impact of such a change in the common law on historic cases in which the *Chan Win–Sui* direction had been given. This made clear that exceptional leave to appeal would need to be sought and only granted where an applicant could demonstrate 'substantial injustice':

> *Moreover, where a conviction has been arrived at by faithfully applying the law as it stood at the time, it can be set aside only by seeking exceptional leave to appeal to the Court of Appeal out of time. That court has power to grant such leave, and may do so if substantial injustice be demonstrated, but it will not do so simply because the law applied has now been declared to have been mistaken. This principle has been consistently applied for many years.*

As noted by Lord Toulson and Lord Hughes, 'substantial injustice' is not a new concept. Lord Hughes had previously extensively considered the test in the 2007 Court of Appeal case of *R*,[4] which concerned a change in the law following the decision of the House of Lords in *Saik*[5] to the effect that in cases of conspiracy to commit offences of money laundering the prosecution was required to prove that the defendant knew that the origins of the funds was unlawful, in contrast to the substantive offences, which required no more than suspicion. The court refused the applications for extensions of time and stated at para. 39:

> *Although Saik shows that the convictions for conspiracy cannot stand, it must have been found by the jury in all cases, or in the case of S he has admitted, that they suspected that the money they handled was illicit. All of them admitted the facts of extensive money-handling.*
>
> *That means that all of them must, on their own cases taken together with the verdicts of the juries, have committed one or more sub-*

4 [2007] 1 Cr.App.R. 10.

5 [2006] UKHL 18.

stantive offences of money laundering, for which suspicion remains the relevant mens rea. Had the law as now explained in Saik been known at their trials, they would no doubt have faced trial on indictments which included at least some substantive charges, and, whether or not convicted of conspiracy, they must have been convicted of substantive offences of great gravity. Whether or not it is now possible to identify such offence(s) and just to substitute convictions for them (as to which see below), this means that subject to any individual grounds for finding substantial injustice, these are strong cases for refusal of leave.

In reviewing earlier authorities, the Court of Appeal considered *inter alia*:

- *Mitchell:*[6] an extension of time was granted on the basis that the applicant was serving a sentence of imprisonment for conduct which, as a result of a later decision of the Court of Appeal, did not amount to an offence.

- *Hawkins:*[7] Referring to the substantial injustice test, Lord Bingham stated:

That practice may on its face seem harsh. On the other hand, the consequences of any other rule are equally unattractive. It would mean that a defendant who had roundly and on advice accepted that he had acted dishonestly and fraudulently, and pleaded guilty, or who had been found guilty and chosen not to appeal could after the event seek to reopen the convictions. If such convictions were to be readily reopened it would be difficult to know where to draw the line or how far to go back.'

Lord Bingham went on to state that, although the general practice is for the court to set its face against reopening convic-

6 [1977] 65 Cr.App.R. 185

7 [1997] 1 Cr.App.R. 234

tions where there has been a change in the law, nonetheless there is no inflexible rule and the court should '*eschew undue technicality*' and consider whether there would be a substantial injustice were leave to appeal not to be granted.

- *Ballinger:*[8] The court refused to extend time in a case where the applicant had been convicted of indecent assault by a Court Martial, in circumstances where the composition of Court Martial was later held to infringe the right to a fair trial under Article 6. This was on the basis that the Applicant had not sought to challenge the conviction until the Article 6 point regarding the structural lack of independence of the trial tribunal had emerged in a subsequent case.

The Application of the 'Substantial Injustice' Test in Joint Enterprise: Johnson

Following *Jogee*, the first set of appeals to come before the Court of Appeal were joined in the case of *Johnson & Ors*[9] and heard by the then Lord Chief Justice, Lord Thomas of Cwmgiedd CJ, the President of the Queen's Bench Division, Sir Brian Leveson and the Vice President of the Criminal Division, Hallett, L.J.

Johnson made plain that an applicant requires 'exceptional leave', and this will only be granted if the applicant can demonstrate that they have suffered 'a substantial injustice' as a consequence of the change in law. The test is one with a 'high threshold'.[10] In determining whether that threshold had been met and therefore substantial injustice, it was necessary to demonstrate that 'the change in the law would, in fact, have made a difference'. The question to be asked was 'Can it therefore be said that there is a sufficiently strong case that the defendant *would*

8 [2005] 2 Cr.App.R. 29

9 [2016] EWCA Crim 1613

10 Para. 20.

not have been convicted of murder if the law had been explained to the jury as set out in *R v Jogee*?'

In determining this question, the court referred at paragraph 21 to consideration of where a case fell on the spectrum of offending:

> *If crime A is a crime of violence which the jury concluded must have involved the use of a weapon so that the inference of participation with an intention to cause really serious harm is strong, that is likely to be very difficult. At the other end of the spectrum, if crime A is a different crime, not involving intended violence or use of force, it may well be easier to demonstrate substantial injustice. The court will also have regard to other matters including whether the applicant was guilty of other, though less serious, criminal conduct.*

As such it is insufficient to demonstrate that the change *might* have made a difference to the verdict or whether the applicant had suffered adverse consequences as a result of a conviction, here almost inevitably a sentence of life imprisonment (the mandatory sentence in cases of murder) or the stigma attached to such a conviction.

The passage of time however is not a relevant consideration in itself:

> *It is not, however, in our view, material to consider the length of time that has elapsed. If there was a substantial injustice, it is irrelevant whether that injustice occurred a short time or a long time ago. It is and remains an injustice.*

Of note and as discussed in subsequent chapters, *Johnson* made clear that '*if the threshold required to justify exceptional leave to appeal is reached, it is likely to be difficult to conclude that the conviction remains safe*'.[11]

11 Para 23.

Attempts to challenge the application of the 'substantial injustice test' have failed. In *Garwood, Miah and Hall,* the applicants sought to appeal further to the Supreme Court. The Court of Appeal however refused to certify a question on the basis that it lacked jurisdiction. In the absence of leave to appeal being granted there was no appeal before the court, merely applications for leave.

It will be noted that there is a circularity to the post-*Jogee* position and substantial injustice test – it is unlikely that the Court of Appeal will grant leave to appeal and yet dismiss the appeal under the safety test. This means that an applicant is in turn is unlikely to be able to surmount the procedural bar necessary to reach the Supreme Court. The only alternative, as posited by Professor Ormorod, would be a leapfrog appeal from a judicial review of a refusal of the CCRC to refer a case based on the fact that the CCRC has misinterpreted the 'substantial injustice' test.

As such, it appears that the substantial injustice test and the hurdles faced by potential applicants are here to stay.

CHAPTER THREE
PREPARING A HISTORIC CASE POST-JOGEE FOR APPEAL

It is increasingly unlikely that cases on appeal will be brought within the relevant time limits (28 days from sentence) and instead cases will continue to most likely require extensions of time, often substantial extensions of time. As such this chapter concentrates on out of time appeals requiring exceptional leave to appeal and therefore engaging the 'substantial injustice' test.

Procedural issues

The first aspect to note is that all of the relevant considerations which generally apply in appeals continue to apply.

There remains a duty on advocates to settle only grounds which are reasonable, have some real prospect of success and are such that the advocate is prepared to argue them before the court. The advocate should not settle grounds he cannot support because he is "instructed" to do so by a defendant[1].

Where instructed as a fresh advocate, the *McCook*[2] principles are likely to be engaged. It is incumbent upon newly instructed advocates to ensure that previous representatives are contacted and that the grounds are sent to ensure that the facts are correct, unless there are in exceptional circumstances good and compelling reasons not to do so.

---

1 *Achogbuo* [2014] EWCA Crim 567; Crim PR CPD IX Appeal 3C.2.

2 [2016] Cr. App. R. 30.

The former Lord Chief Justice, Lord Thomas significantly modified the *McCook* obligations in the case of *Grant-Murray; McGill*[3] to require newly instructed counsel to:

i. make all proper and diligent enquires of previous counsel, advocates and solicitors, so that they have all the information properly to understand what took place prior to and during the trial;

ii. then expressly certify in the grounds of application for leave to appeal submitted to the court on form NG that that has been done. The Court will not entertain an application without such a certification.

iii. identify for previous lawyers the issues that relate to the conduct of the trial which are relevant to the appeal. Specific questions must be formulated and specifically put.

iv. In other cases there will be implicit criticism; in such a case there can be no shying away from putting fairly and squarely the implicit criticism of those then acting for the Applicant at the trial so that the appellate court has all the information before it when it commences the consideration of the application.

v. The fact that a trial lawyer might have retired or left the profession to take up office or for some other reason does not excuse the newly instructed advocate from pursuing such inquiries with that person

Ancillary to this, the Court may also require a waiver of privilege, at least in part.

---

3 [2017] EWCA Crim 1228.

It is important to note that the principles set out in *James*[4] will apply if there are any proposed amendments to grounds or where a renewal is being considered:

i. As a general rule, all the Grounds of Appeal an applicant wishes to advance should be lodged with the Notice of Appeal/ Application;

ii. The 'section 31' stage is an important stage in the process and should not be 'bypassed.' solely on the basis that fresh representatives would have done or argued things differently from the trial lawyers;

iii. Applications to advance fresh Grounds that have not in been considered by the single Judge must be accompanied by an application to "vary" the notice of appeal;

The full Court will take into account a number of factors when deciding whether to allow the application to vary the Grounds of Appeal. These include the extent of the delay in advancing the new ground(s), the reason for the delay in advancing the new ground(s) and whether the issues or facts giving rise to the new grounds were known to the applicant's representative at the time he or she advised the applicant.

The principles relating to loss of time apply; however, it does not appear that the power has been exercised in cases litigating non-compliant *Jogee* directions. This may reflect the fact that relatively few applications for leave to appeal have reached the full court and further that, where they have, the ambit, scope and impact of the judgement in *Jogee* have been considered. However, this does not mean that the Court will not do so in future appeals, and potentially without warning to the appellant or their representatives.

---

4 [2018] EWCA Crim 285.

More generally, in *Gray & Ors*[5], the Vice President of the Court of Appeal Criminal Division, Lady Justice Hallett, observed that:

> [T]he only means the court has of discouraging unmeritorious applications which waste precious time and resources is by using the powers given to us by Parliament in the Criminal Appeal Act 1968 and the Prosecution of Offences Act 1985.

At the Single Judge stage, the Judge can initial the relevant box on Form SJ to indicate that the full court consider making a loss of time order. Irrespective of whether the single Judge initials the box, the full Court can still consider making such an order if they take the view that the application is wholly without merit. The fact of legal representation and advice, along with the settling of grounds by legal advisors does not preclude such an order. Where the box is initialled, representations can be made on Form SJ (Renewal form (Part 3A)).

It is likely that any application based on a non-compliant *Jogee* direction will be referred to the full court for consideration, essentially bypassing the single Judge leave stage.

Approaching a potential appeal

As an initial consideration, it will be necessary to establish whether any appeal against conviction has previously been lodged, considered or abandoned before the Court. This will inform whether or not the correct procedure is an application to the Criminal Cases Review Commission or the Court of Appeal, Criminal Division. Similarly, it can be helpful to ascertain whether any co-accused has appealed and if so, obtain the judgements. These can contain valuable insights into the issues before the Court, how the matters were put and factual conclusions at sentence.

5 [2014] EWCA Crim 2372.

The following applies equally to the preparation of either an application to the CCRC or to the Court of Appeal.

The first stage is to identify if it is indeed a case which engages principles of parasitic accessorial liability and as a consequence offends *Jogee.* In the authors' experience, many cases seeking advice post-conviction do not actually engage the limited issues raised in the Supreme Court decision in *Jogee.* They may, for example actually involve the scenario where more than one defendant is said to be a principal and at trial the case has been put squarely on the basis that the defendants are joint principals. This would arise for example in a case where two or more individuals take part in a joint attack, both stabbing and contributing to the death of the deceased. Furthermore, a number of Judges were in practice giving *Jogee* compliant directions in advance of the Supreme Court ruling. In such situations, the case has never been left to the jury on the basis of foresight, instead requiring a shared intention. In reality the number of cases in which there is a viable appeal will be limited.

It will be necessary to consider the summing up, jury directions and route to verdict in detail. Firstly, to ascertain the basis on which the case was put but also how it was left to the jury. It is however clear that a non-compliant *Jogee* direction on foresight alone will be insufficient to found a successful appeal. As such, advisors will need to consider the prosecution case in detail; how it was opened, how it was put in cross-examination or to relevant witnesses and the basis of liability urged upon the jury in the Crown's closing speech.

In addition, the evidential and factual conclusions will need to be looked at closely, along with the general developments within the trial[6].

The starting point based on the caselaw to date indicates that it will be necessary to demonstrate that the case was one predicated on foresight. In such circumstances, directions also providing an alternative basis of conviction based on a shared intention may not prove fatal.

---

6 *James* [2018] EWCA 285.

Most recently, Mrs Justice Cheema-Grubb, has sought to provide a checklist of sorts relating to practical assistance in litigating post *Jogee* appeals.[7] In doing so she identified '5 keys' to unlocking the appeal[8], which are set out in bold followed by our comments:

1. **Preparation of a clear chronology** which cross- references to the rest of the material in the appeal bundle.

2. **Gather all relevant judicial material** e.g. the written legal directions (or a transcript of them) and the Route to Verdict. Note in particular the diligence and care required by advocates considering pursuing grounds of appeal said to have been missed by trial lawyers. If privilege is waived, an Advice on Appeal provided at conviction may be extremely helpful.

3. **Provide 'sufficient but not necessarily comprehensive notes of the way the case was opened, the relevant prosecution evidence for the Crown at trial, the relevant defence evidence if any and at the very least, the factual summing up'**. A note of caution was sounded on the obtaining of transcripts owing to limited resources. In particular, if relevant the applicant's evidence should be supplied (with relevant sections highlighted and referenced). It was noted by Cheema-Grubb, J., that this formed an important part of *Crilly*[9], with the judgement referring to and quoting significant passages.

4. **Provide an analysis of how the change of law would have made a difference to the directions and questions for the jury to resolve.** This was described by Cheema-Grubb, J., as being at

7 Cheema-Grubb (2018), 'Keynote Speech', *Criminal Bar Association Winter Conference*, 24 November, available at < https://www.judiciary.uk/wp-content/uploads/2018/12/CBA-WINTER-CONFERENCE-2018-KEYNOTE-SPEECH.pdf >.

8 Ibid, paras 10-15.

9 [2018] EWCA Crim 168.

the heart of any application for appeal against conviction. This requires an analysis of the factual findings as set against the jury directions. In multi-handed cases this requires a realistic assessment of the type of crime envisaged as compared to what actually happened. This did not involve impermissible speculation about the jury's reasoning but a considered forensic analysis. Referring to *Crilly*, it was noted that 'the crucial and valuable distinction between the way the case was put against him as opposed to his co- defendants, won the day'.

5. **Encapsulate the continuing impact of the conviction**. No real guidance was provided in relation to cases of murder, with Cheema-Grubb, J., simply stating that it '*may be self-evident in murder cases, or where the sentence is still being served*'. This may be a reflection of the fact that (in the authors' view) the test for substantial injustice and safety appear to be elided in such cases with a narrow construction applied.

Whilst of some assistance, the '5 keys' are necessarily limited and invariably provide little actual insight into the principles to be applied as opposed to the groundwork of an appeal.

Turning to broader considerations and applying the principles to date, the following will need to be considered when approaching any appeal post-Jogee.

i. How the case was left to the jury with regard to the basis for criminal liability:

    a. Summing up

    b. The directions to the jury regarding:

        1. Joint enterprise/venture;

        2. The scope of any joint plan/venture;

        3. Intention;

4. Foresight;

ii. Whether or not there were alternative bases for conviction e.g. both a shared intention and foresight in the alternative;

iii. If so, the way the case was actually placed before the jury;

iv. Any factual conclusions that could be drawn from the directions/route to verdict;

v. The basis on which the Crown put the case against the prospective applicant. This will include consideration of:

   a. the Crown's opening;

   b. cross-examination of the prospective applicant (where evidence was given);

   c. cross-examination of any co-accused; and

   d. closing speeches.

vi. If crime A becomes crime B, where crime A falls on the *Johnson* spectrum and what inferences can be drawn and the strength of any support for said inference;[10]

vii. Any additional factors supporting the argument that the substantial injustice test is met. At present a broader approach has not found favour however arguably the issue extends beyond a singular analysis as to whether a *Jogee* compliant direction would have made a difference. Such considerations may include age, vulnerability, the principle of fair labelling etc;

viii. Potentially consideration of conditional intent (this appears to be the general approach of the Crown in resisting such appeals);

---

10 See *Johnson* at §21

ix. Consideration of any previous advice on appeal and the views of the previous legal team;

x. Where there appear to be merits and grounds are settled, then compliance with *McCook* as modified.

It is clear from this list that the work involved in submitting an appeal on the basis of Jogee is arduous. There is a lack of consistency in the Court of Appeal's judgments and it is unclear why some some small number of cases have succeeded when other very similar cases have not. In the next chapters we look at what can be learnt from both the successful and unsuccessful appeals.

CHAPTER FOUR
POST-JOGEE: SUCCESSFUL APPEALS AGAINST CONVICTION

Unsurprisingly, the concerns regarding floodgates have not come to pass. Since 2016, there have been only **two** successful appeals in the wake of *Jogee*. These were the cases of *Dresner*[1] and *Crilly*.[2]

The Court of Appeal in each matter directed a re-trial. Both subsequently resulted in acceptable pleas of guilty to manslaughter at the directed re-trial.

Dreszer was an in-time appeal. *Crilly* required an extension of time, engaging the principles outlined in *Johnson*[3], including the 'substantial injustice' test. *Crilly* remains the only case to have been granted 'exceptional' leave to appeal. The 'substantial injustice' test has been effective in closing off any realistic avenue of appeal for almost all those affected by the decades long error in law arising out of the decision in *Chan-Wing-Siu*.

Set against that, misconceptions remain as to general understanding of the principles of joint enterprise and the extent to which *Jogee* changed the law. This has resulted in a number of cases coming before the Court of Appeal which have not realistically engaged the issue of parasitic accessorial liability or where foresight has been treated as authorisation for intent.

---

1 [2018] EWCA Crim 454.

2 [2018] EWCA Crim 168.

3 [2017] 1 Cr App R 12.

The following section considers *Dreszer* and *Crilly* and principles to be distilled from the Court of Appeal judgments. It is worth going into some detail on the cases because of what they tell us about how the Court interprets

The case of *Kamil Dreszer*

On or about 21 September 2010 Andrezj Kulesza, a Polish national, was killed. His dismembered and decomposed body was not discovered until 25 April 2011 in a field near Northampton. The body was in such a state of decomposition that experts could not identify the cause of death.

The Prosecution case was that the death took place against a backdrop of drugs debt. They alleged that five men had been responsible for the death: Misiak, Janik, Koswoski, Lapinski and Dreszer. The deceased owed money to Misiak, a drug dealer. As a consequence, he had been kidnapped and falsely imprisoned in a flat in London which was occupied by Misiak and Dreszer. Demands for money were made. The deceased had telephoned and texted his girlfriend, asking for money. Those contemporaneous messages stated that he was being held, had been tortured for the last two days and asked for money, in the absence of which he believed that he would be killed.

Evidence of what had taken place in the flat between 19 and 21 September 2010 came from the girlfriend of Misiak. She described seeing a sheet covered in blood which Misiak told her to tidy up. She had heard the appellant, amongst others, in the living room and it sounded as if someone was being beaten up. She had then heard Misiak and Dreszer dragging someone into the loft, sounds of an assault and screaming. On 21 September she had seen Misiak and Dreszer and others in the living room, along with a man who looked as though he had been assaulted. She had then left and returned after work later that day and found Dreszer and another removing items, cleaning and painting.

A forensic examination revealed two spots of the deceased's blood on the inside of the door to the loft, and one spot on the living-room side of the living-room door.

Dreszer gave no account in interview of his involvement. Initially he lied and then he answered 'no comment'.

The case had a lengthy procedural history with Dreszer initially being convicted of murder, kidnapping, false imprisonment and preventing a lawful and decent burial of a body in 2013. With regard to the co-accused, Misiak was killed in a car accident in 2012 and so was not tried. The other three all stood trial, Janik was acquitted of murder, but convicted of manslaughter, kidnapping, false imprisonment and preventing a lawful burial; Koswoski was acquitted of murder but convicted of preventing a lawful burial; and Lapinski was also acquitted of murder.

At the trial in 2013 the Prosecution sought to leave the case to the jury on the basis that Dreszer, along with the others had actively participated in the fatal attack on the deceased but that in the alternative, was guilty on the basis of joint participation in the offence of false imprisonment, with the foresight that one of the others involved might intentionally kill or seriously injure the deceased. The Judge refused to allow the latter basis to be left. This was based on pragmatic reasons concerning effective case management with the Judge fearing an over complication of the issues before the jury given the number of defendants and offences on the indictment. As a consequence, legal directions were limited to the first basis of criminal liability. During jury deliberations however a question was asked raising the spectre of criminal liability attaching through foresight. Directions in this regard were given. The jury had however not been addressed on this basis previously and Dreszer had lost the benefit of dealing with this point before the jury. As a consequence the conviction was appealed.

The conviction for murder was overturned by the Court of Appeal in 2014.[4] Following the re-trial in 2016, Dreszer was again convicted of murder. Dreszer did not give evidence at either of his trials.

At the re-trial, the jury were directed on two possible bases for criminal liability;

i. that he intended as part of a joint plan that the deceased should be assaulted with an intent to kill or cause really serious injury;

ii. accessorial liability (foresight) in that he realised that there was a real possibility that someone in the course of a joint plan might assault Mr Kulesza with intent to kill or cause him really serious injury.

The appeal[5] focused on the misdirection in law concerning secondary liability, following *Jogee.*

The relevant directions given were:

> *Secondary party murder, count 1. For the defendant to be guilty of murder as a secondary party, the prosecution must prove so that you are sure:*
>
> *(a) there was a joint plan with Misiak, in the course of which Andrezj Kulesza was murdered by the principal party.*
>
> *(b) the defendant agreed to participate and was participating in the joint plan at the time of the killing.*
>
> *(c) …*

4 See, *Dreszer* [2014] EWCA Crim 2426

5 Heard by Treacy, LJ., King, J., and Andrew Baker, J.

> (i) *He either intended that at least one of those participating in the joint plan would assault Andrezj Kulesza in the course of it, with intent to kill him or cause him really serious injury, or*
>
> (ii) *realised that there was a real possibility that, in the course of the joint plan, at least one of those then participating in it might assault Andrezj Kulesza, with intent to kill him or cause him really serious injury.*
>
> *I deal with (a) and, in particular, the requirement that, in the course of the joint plan, Andrezj Kulesza was murdered by the principal party. Was the principal party guilty of murdering Andrezj Kulesza?*
>
> *You cannot convict the defendant of murder as a secondary party unless you are sure the principal party, whoever he was, was guilty of murder.*

The Judge went on to provide directions on secondary party manslaughter:

> *If you are sure of (a) and (b) above but not (c), you should consider the offence of manslaughter. For the defendant to be guilty of manslaughter as a secondary party the prosecution must prove so that you are sure:*
>
> (d) *There was a joint plan with Misiak and/or Janek in the course of which Andrezj Kulesza was unlawfully killed.*
>
> (e) *The defendant agreed to participate and was participating in the joint plan at the time of the killing.*
>
> (f) *The defendant realised that at least one of those participating in the joint plan might assault Andrezj Kulesza in the course of it, as a result of which he might suffer some injury, but you consider that he did not realise or may not have realised that such an*

assault would be carried out, with intent to kill Andrezj Kulesza or cause him really serious injury.

If you are sure of (d), (e) and (f) above your verdict will be guilty of manslaughter.

The route to verdict mirrored the directions:

a. *Are you sure that Andrezj Kulesza was unlawfully killed in the course of a joint plan? If no, your verdicts are not guilty on counts 1 and 2. If yes, go to question 2.*

b. *Are you sure that the defendant was participating in the joint plan at the time of the killing? If no, your verdicts are not guilty on counts 1 and 2. If yes, go to question 3.*

c. *Are you sure that the principal party murdered Andrezj Kulesza? If yes, go to question 4. If no, go to question 5. [This was modified following a jury question].*

d. *Are you sure that, in participating in the joint plan, the defendant either:*

   i. *intended that at least one of those then participating in it should assault Andrezj Kulesza, intending to kill him or cause him really serious injury or*

   ii. *realised there was a real possibility that at least one of those then participating in might assault Andrezj Kulesza, intending to kill him or cause him really serious injury? If yes, your verdict is guilty of murder. If no, your verdict is not guilty of murder, and go to question 5.*

A number of complaints were made. The Court rejected each before proceeding to the core issue as to whether the conviction had been rendered unsafe by reason of the misdirection. It was accepted by the Court that there had been a misdirection (*Jogee*); however the Court reminded itself of the observation in Johnson (at §9) that 'even in relation to in time appeals, the fact that the jury were correctly directed in accordance with the then prevailing law does not automatically render the verdict unsafe'.

The Court held that:

i. There had been a misdirection in law;

ii. The directions expressly stated that it was for the jury to determine whether there was a joint plan and, if so, its scope;

iii. The jury were directed on participation in a joint plan to assault (which was defined as the unlawful use of force against another person);

iv. There was a failure to couple this with the additional requirement that such assault took place with the intention of causing at least really serious injury (intention direction);

v. The directions failed to define the scope of the joint plan in terms of intention nor were the jury asked to resolve the scope of the joint plan (the defence submission was that the plan extended no further than to kidnap and falsely imprison with a view to recovering the drug debt);

vi. As a consequence the jury were directed that they could convict of manslaughter as a secondary party if they were sure that he had realised that a participant in a joint plan to assault might assault the deceased, causing some injury;

vii. With regard to the route to verdict:

a. Questions 1 and 2 were concerned with ascertaining criminal liability for any form of homicide (murder/manslaughter);

b. Questions 3, 4 and 5 sought to draw the boundary between murder and manslaughter;

   i. Question 4 delineated the bases upon either of which the jury, if sure, could convict of murder.

   ii. Question 5 posed accurately the questions to ask, if it was not murder, before the jury could convict of manslaughter.

It was clear that 'On the basis of the judge's directions and, following his route to verdict, the jury had to answer the questions posed at question 4. Such a course clearly admitted of the possibility that the jury might not be sure that the jury (sic) had the necessary intention shown at 4(a), but did have the foresight shown at paragraph 4(b)'.

Turning to the facts of the case, the Court considered the following to be of import when considering the safety of the conviction:

i. There was no witness to the actual killing;

ii. The Crown could not specify what had caused the death or where it had occurred;

iii. The case therefore depended on inferences which could be drawn from the evidence.

iv. In those circumstances, this was not the sort of case where the Court could have any confidence that the jury must have convicted on the basis of intention as opposed to foresight.

v. The Court accepted that this was a case where the evidence available might well have led to a conclusion that Dreszer participated with the necessary intention that the deceased should be caused at least serious physical harm; however noted that the judge at trial had considered it appropriate to leave the matter to the jury on the basis of foresight.

vi. As such, the trial Judge had not ruled out the possibility of conviction on the basis of foresight.

vii. Neither could the Court of Appeal.

viii. As such, the misdirection could not be overlooked and the conviction was unsafe.

A re-trial was ordered. In the course of this, the Court commented that the case was an evidentially strong one.

The (second) re-trial was listed in October 2019. On the first day, Mr Dreszer entered a guilty plea to manslaughter. He was subsequently sentenced to 12 years and 9 months.

It is clear that there was a misdirection in law and that Dreszer may have been convicted on this erroneous basis. This in itself should be sufficient to found a successful appeal, however as discussed, this is not the position.

The decision of the trial Judge to leave the case to the jury on the alternative basis of foresight was considered by the Court of Appeal to be an important factor in their consideration of the appeal, indicating that at trial the Judge considered that it was possible that the jury could convict on this basis and consequently they also could not rule this out. This has not been a consideration in the majority of post *Jogee* appeals. The decision and reasoning sits unhappily with an analysis of other out of time appeals (as discussed below). This was not a classic PAL case, with crime A being one of non-violence, later leading to crime B. The evidence supporting a joint intention to cause really serious harm was strong. There was ample evidence that Dreszer was an active participant at the very least in the kidnap and false imprisonment of the deceased over a prolonged period of time. He had been convicted of these offences by the jury. There was evidence that during this time the deceased had been assaulted (in the deceased's terms 'tortured'), while threats were made to recover a drug debt. Dreszer had been present at various points of his detention and assisted in forcing him into the attic where sounds of an assault were then heard. He had also been involved in the clean-up operation, which included painting. The decision of the Court of Appeal to quash the conviction is, when one considers the appeals dismissed, a surprising one and difficult to reconcile with other cases.

The case of *Crilly*

Crilly[6] was an out of time appeal, requiring exceptional leave under the 'substantial injustice' test. In 2005, Crilly was convicted of the robbery and murder of 71-year-old Mr Maduemezia (the deceased).

The Crown alleged that he, along with two others, Flynn and Gaffney had broken into Mr Maduemezia's flat to burgle the property. It was common ground that all three had longstanding drug addictions and that their habits were supported by committing dwelling house burglaries.

During the course of the burglary, Mr Maduemezia was hit to the head at least once with a blow of moderate force, causing him to fall and hit his head resulting in a fatal injury. A post-mortem revealed bruising to the face and subdural haemorrhage, consistent with a blow and then striking the head upon falling. The deceased was found dead a few days later by a neighbour. His body was on the floor, with his jumper pulled

6 [2018] EWCA Crim 168.

up over his head. A tie had been tightened around his neck and required cutting off. In addition his body had been searched.

The property had also been subjected to a prolonged and systematic search and a telephone socket had been pulled from the wall with a degree of force. The deceased's blood was found on Crilly's footwear and imprints matching his footwear were found in the property.

Flynn was convicted of the murder of Mr Maduemezia on the basis that he was the principal. He had inflicted the fatal punch and in so doing, intended to kill or cause really serious harm. Crilly was convicted on the basis of secondary liability.

It was the defence case that the group had sought to ascertain that the property was unoccupied with Crilly's role being to knock on the door prior to entry. Unfortunately Mr Maduemezia had a hearing impairment and as such there was no answer. The group broke in to find Mr Maduemezia present. Flynn had shouted and demanded money. Crilly shouted "Let's leave, let's fucking go." This was ignored by Flynn who pushed Mr Maduemezia back into the chair as he tried to stand up. Crilly again suggested that they leave the property however Flynn was adamant that there was money in the property. Crilly and Gaffney then went to search a bedroom. On their return to the living room, they informed Flynn that they had not found anything causing Flynn to become angrier. When Mr Maduemezia tried to stand again, Flynn punched him once to the left side of his face, causing him to fall. Crilly assisted Mr Maduemezia back on to his feet and into the chair and again shouted that they should leave. Crilly then left alone and waited for the other two for around ten minutes. They appeared with a food blender which they subsequently sold. All then went to their respective homes.

In interview Crilly made no comment.

There was no real issue that Crilly was guilty of a robbery. In evidence, Crilly accepted as much and in closing submissions to the jury the defence did not suggest that he should be acquitted of that count. Crilly had given evidence that he had gone to the property with the others as part of a joint plan to burgle. He had realized that the homeowner was present and that it had quickly progressed to a robbery. He had attempted to get the other two to leave however he had made the choice to stay and continue with the offence. Crilly accepted that there were problems with the homeowner being present and further that as the offence progressed that Mr Maduemezia might put up resistance and the situation get out of control. He had seen Flynn both push and later punch Mr Maduemezia. Crilly also accepted that he had foreseen the possibility that Flynn would cause really serious harm to the deceased but stated that he didn't really think that Flynn would hit an elderly man and did not expect the level of violence to go as far as it did.

The prosecution case as left to the jury was that the men were a party to an assault with intent to rob. The perpetrator of the violence intended to kill or cause grievous (really serious) bodily harm and his accomplice or accomplices had either the same intent or foresight that grievous bodily harm would be caused and intended. The jury was directed on the erroneous law as it was understood pre *Jogee*.

Of note however, in the route to verdict, the second question asked the jury whether they were sure:

> *[T]hat as part of the joint enterprise to rob Mr Maduemezia unlawful force was used upon him and which caused his death and whoever used that force intended to cause really serious bodily injury and at the time of using that force John Crilly had intended that he should suffer really serious bodily injury or realise that there was a risk that force would be used against him with the intention that he be caused really serious bodily injury.*

The erroneous direction comprised the sole ground of appeal against conviction.

The grounds submitted that it would 'be difficult to find a case in which the issue of foresight was of greater relevance to the ultimate verdict and therefore the judgment in *Jogee* [was] particularly relevant to [Crilly's] case'.

The court went on to state that the:

> *[E]ssence of the case therefore was that whatever the nature of the original criminal enterprise, the threats and violence at the scene in order to steal amounted to robbery. When the defendant continued to participate in the offence of robbery, aware that it was a realistic possibility that Flynn would cause serious harm to the victim (in the light of his previous convictions and previous character), the defendant was guilty of murder on the basis of joint enterprise.*

Further, applying both *Jogee* and *Johnson*, 'had the jury been directed in accordance with the principles as set out in *Jogee* it **would** have made a difference to the jury's approach' (emphasis added).

In support of this, the defence relied on seven facts:

i. The murder took place in the course of a joint enterprise that began as a burglary for which no weapons were carried;

ii. The presence of the deceased in the premises was not expected when the Crilly entered.

iii. There was no settled intention to rob when they entered the flat. Thereafter the event was a fast moving one and the burglary converted into a robbery;

iv. Crilly urged his co-accused to leave the premises when they found the victim in the living room (this was based on his own account);

v. Crilly was guilty of robbery because he remained part of the joint enterprise once it had begun. However, he was not one of those who was accused of using or threatening force;

vi. The victim was killed by at least one moderately forceful blow to the head by his co-accused.

vii. The cross-examination of Crilly by the Prosecution was to the effect that the defendant was aware of the real possibility that Flynn would cause really serious harm to the deceased with the requisite intent but nevertheless continued to participate in the offence. It was not put to him he intended really serious bodily harm.

In addition the Court was taken to the relevant parts of Crilly's evidence dealing with foresight and the summing up. As set out above, the Judge directed the jury on the basis of parasitic accessorial liability as it was then understood: namely that the jury had to determine whether there was a joint enterprise, including Crilly and Flynn, to commit robbery using violence against Mr Maduemezia should he resist. In relation to anyone participating in the robbery but who did not hit the victim the judge directed the jury that they would be guilty of murder if:

> *'[F]orce was used by those taking part in the robbery with the intention of causing really serious bodily injury and you are sure that these two either at the very least realised there was a real risk that force would be used against him with that intention, namely cause really serious bodily injury and this force caused death.'*

With regard to the route to verdict and in particular the potential difficulties presented on appeal in the second question contained in the route to verdict, it was submitted that court should approach the case on the basis upon which it was put to the jury, namely foresight.

Set against this the Prosecution submitted that:

i. The direction to the jury represented a correct statement of law as it was then understood;

ii. The deceased was in the flat when Crilly and his fellow offenders entered;

iii. The deceased was 71 years of age, alone and unable to offer resistance against three men;

iv. On the defendant's account, Flynn confronted the deceased and became increasingly aggressive;

v. Flynn had previous convictions of violent robbery and Crilly foresaw that he would be likely to use force upon the deceased (It is worth noting that Crilly disputed knowing the detail of these convictions);

vi. Although Crilly was reluctant to concede in cross-examination that force was likely to be used, it was open to the jury to conclude that such force would be of a nature that was likely to cause grievous bodily harm;

vii. Despite that knowledge Crilly continued in the robbery and went on searching the house;

viii. He was present when Flynn struck the deceased. His continued participation demonstrated a willingness to continue in a joint enterprise where serious violence may be used by a man with a history of serious violence and a man who was becoming increasingly angry;

ix. Crilly was caught out in a series of lies which he told before and during the trial and the jury was therefore entitled to reject his account. The jury was entitled to reject and must have rejected any suggestion that he did not foresee that the force might be used with the intention to cause grievous bodily harm;

x. Crilly was unable to explain: why the deceased's tie was so tight and had to be cut off; why there was a contact smear of blood on his trainer; how the deceased suffered the fatal injury; why he ended up in the middle of the room away from the sofa; why the table and chairs were overturned; why there were three sets of footprints in the bedroom when on his account only he and Gaffney had entered the room and why a neighbour heard the sound of something heavy being moved in the flat;

xi. As such, that there was ample evidence from which the jury was entitled to conclude that the robbery of the deceased, to which the defendant had pleaded not guilty but eventually admitted, was one carried out in circumstances where it was understood by the participants that if any resistance was offered sufficient force would be used to render him incapable of resistance and that would include force with the intention of causing grievous bodily harm;

xii. Finally, the test of substantial injustice was not met. The offence of robbery (crime A) was a crime of violence, albeit not at the upper end of the spectrum as discussed in *Johnson*.

In considering the case, the Court derived the following principles from *Jogee* and *Johnson*, which form a helpful blueprint for future appeals:

i. To qualify for the grant of exceptional leave the defendant must establish a 'substantial injustice' would be caused if it was denied. The fact that there has been a change in the law is not in itself sufficient where a person was properly convicted on the law as it stood at the time of trial, as here;

ii. The threshold for demonstrating a substantial injustice is a high one;

iii. In determining whether that high threshold has been met the court will have regard to the strength of the case advanced, that a change in the law would in fact have made a difference.

Applying those principles to the facts proved problematic. The Court considered that there were few factual findings that could be distilled from the verdicts and possibly only two: The defendant was guilty of robbery and at the very least he foresaw that grievous bodily harm might be caused to the victim of the robbery yet continued to participate in it. It was not possible to ascertain whether or not the jury found that the plan was to burgle an unoccupied (as per Crilly's account) or occupied premises.

With this in mind, the Court considered that the most likely scenario was a planned burglary of an unoccupied dwelling house and not a robbery, with no violence initially intended. When the victim did not hear the doorbell the situation changed. When Flynn attacked Mr Maduemezia, the defendant continued to participate in the robbery despite having the foresight that Flynn would cause Mr Maduemezia really serious bodily harm with the intention of doing so. This was the basis upon which the case was presented to the jury. Of note, this was considered also to be the fairest scenario for the purpose of the appeal.

A distinction could be drawn between the position of Crilly and Flynn, with Crilly not being accused of initially intending or foreseeing any violence, inflicting any violence or intending to cause grievous bodily harm. The court pointed to the short period of time between realizing Mr Maduemezia was present and the conversion of the burglary into a robbery with the infliction of violence. Furthermore the violence actually used was relatively limited to potentially a push and a punch.

The Court considered the spectrum of offences as identified in *Johnson*[7] but found that the facts (as the Court considered it was obliged to take them) did not fit easily. The Court ultimately concluded that the robbery fell between the middle to lower end of the spectrum. In discussion, the Court held that where crime A was a burglary of an unoccupied dwelling the offence would 'undoubtedly fall easily into the lower end of the spectrum'. Here, however crime A was the robbery. It did not fall at the upper end of the spectrum owing to the lack of a weapon carried to the scene, the fact that any joint enterprise involving the threat or use of force was formed at the very last moment and the physical violence was limited. Equally however the offence of robbery was not one at the lower end of the spectrum, including as it must the threat or use of force.

In considering the substantial injustice test, the Court considered that the 'case against the defendant was to all intents and purposes a case about his foresight'. In the circumstances, the 'evidence against him was not so strong that we can safely and fairly infer the jury would have found the requisite intent to cause really serious bodily harm had the issue been left to them by the judge'.

Re-trial or substitution of a conviction for manslaughter?

Dreszer and Crilly both sought the quashing of their convictions for murder and the substitution of a conviction for manslaughter. In doing so, they resisted an order for a re-trial. Submissions focused on the

7 At para 21: "In determining whether that high threshold has been met the court will primarily and ordinarily have regard to the strength of the case advanced that the change in the law would in fact have made a difference. If crime A is a crime of violence which the jury concluded must have involved the use of a weapon so that the inference of participation with intention to cause really serious harm was strong that is likely to be very difficult. At the other end of the spectrum if crime A is a different crime not involving intended violence or use of force it may well be easier to demonstrate substantial injustice. The court will also have regard to other matters including whether the [defendant] was guilty of other less serious criminal conduct."

passage of time, history of proceedings and time served in custody which would be appropriate or broadly commensurate with a conviction for manslaughter. Set against this, the Prosecution sought a re-trial on the basis of strong public interest and the seriousness of the case. In both cases, the Prosecution's submissions were accepted by the Court, with the Court also commenting on the evidential strength of the cases.

Both judgments were subject to restrictions, so as not to prejudice the impending re-trials. These reporting restrictions have now been lifted.

Principles to be drawn

It is difficult to distill any guiding principles from the successful cases on appeal, not least because there remain only two. What is clear, is that the Court of Appeal has maintained the approach as set out in *Johnson*; there has been no relaxing of the high threshold as found in the 'substantial injustice' test. Although 'substantial injustice' and the 'safety' test were addressed separately in the judgments, it is clear that the factors which would found substantial injustice will also undermine the safety of the conviction. Safety as a separate concept is dealt with briefly and by reference back to those issues concerning substantial injustice within the judgments. In summary, the issue will be whether *Jogee* compliant directions **would** have made a difference.

Unsurprisingly, both successful appeals engaged PAL principles with crime A turning into crime B. The guidance in *Johnson*[8] on the spectrum of offences provides some assistance as to the strength of any inferences which can be drawn as to participation with intention to cause really serious bodily harm. It is axiomatic that the lower crime A falls on that spectrum, the more likely the Court will be to consider that substantial injustice has arisen.

8 Para 21.

In both *Crilly* and *Dreszer* there was no evidence of use of a weapon. *Crilly* was a classic PAL case in that the initial offence was one of non-violence (burglary) where the offenders had taken measures to ascertain whether the premises was unoccupied but where it turned out to be occupied. It had then transformed very rapidly into a robbery and subsequently resulted in the murder of the occupier. The violence used was not excessive and did not sit easily with a conclusion of either an intention to kill or cause really serious harm. There was also an attempt to stop the violence and to withdraw; however, this was exclusively based on the defence account with no apparent corroboration. It is perhaps surprising that the court considered the case on that factual basis, where the account was derived from a defendant, when considering the Court of Appeal's earlier approach to defence versions of events in the *Johnson* cases.

The extent of any violence is likely to be critical. In *Dreszer* there was uncertainty over the cause or mechanism of death; although there was evidence of an assault on more than one occasion and inferences could be drawn. In *Crilly* the violence was limited.

Directions as to the scope of any joint plan are likely to be relevant. The absence of such direction or jury decision on these points being relied upon by the Court in *Dreszer*. This can be contrasted with other cases where the generic basic jury direction on joint venture and fundamental difference have been considered sufficient to dispose of any issue.[9]

The Court considered it to be of significance that the case in *Crilly* was put to the jury on the basis of foresight, notwithstanding that an intention direction had also been part of the route to verdict. The latter did not prove fatal to the appeal. The Prosecution had nailed its colours to the mast. In this regard emphasis was placed on not only the directions, but also on conducting a forensic approach to the evidence in the case including that of the cross-examination of the defendant.

9 See for example *Worgan*, 2019, unreported

The approach however conflicts with other cases, for example *Grant-Murray and Henry; McGill, Hewitt and Hewitt* [2017] EWCA 1228 where, the case was put against a 13 year old child on the basis of foresight alone both in the prosecution opening, throughout cross-examination, closing speeches and summing up and yet the appeal was dismissed almost summarily by the Court with little to no analysis. Instead the Court was satisfied that the jury would have found intention. The position is far from reconcilable.

Interestingly, the inclusion of the foresight direction in the route to verdict as a basis upon which to found criminal liability to murder was also relied on heavily in *Dreszer*; however this has appeared to carry little, if any, weight in other cases, even as an indication of the trial Judge's views. Furthermore it is inherent within any appeal based on *Jogee* that the foresight direction must have been given as a potential alternative (or primary basis) for conviction or there would be no possibility of an appeal based on the misdirection in law.

Neither judgment considers directly the issue of conditional intent, despite there being a clear potential evidential basis for such a contention; the Prosecution in Crilly advanced such a proposition. This contrasts to the approach taken in other cases. It is unclear whether the Court simply failed to grapple with the concept or considered it to not apply (given the apparent acceptance of the defence account as the factual basis of the appeal). Conditional intent of course remains an intent. Foresight there would be insufficient. To approach it in any other way would be to fall into the trap of treating foresight as authorization for intention and return to a pre-*Jogee* position. At some stage, there will no doubt be full argument on conditional intention and its relationship to *Jogee* and *Johnson*.

At the end of the day, when these decisions are looked at carefully, the overarching conclusion is simple. The decisions to date are ultimately of limited assistance and no doubt will be considered fact specific by the Court of Appeal.

CHAPTER FIVE
POST-JOGEE: UNSUCCESSFUL APPEALS AGAINST CONVICTION

With the exception of two successful appeals as previously discussed, all applications for leave to appeal out of time have been refused. The following provides a summary compendium of the reported decisions to date to provide guidance and insights into scenarios which have not been deemed to give rise to substantial injustice or undermine the safety of the conviction. It concentrates on cases of homicide.

The case of *Lansana*[1][2]

In May 2015, Lansana and a co-accused, Agera were convicted of robbery and murder. Both had previously pleaded guilty to conspiracy to commit burglary. Two others were acquitted of murder. They had previously burgled an empty flat in the expectation of substantial cash being stored there. This was not located and they returned the following day in a further attempt to locate it. This was abandoned. As the defendants and others drove away, they passed the deceased and his father approaching a bus stop. On the Prosecution's case the defendants and one other got out of the car with the intention of robbing the men. Lansana had a bag and before they approached the men there was some activity at the car boot. The incident was primarily captured on CCTV. The men were approached from behind and during the course of the attack, the deceased received two serious knife wounds: one was to prove fatal. The attackers made off having taken the deceased's watch and bag. The knife used in the attack was a large hunting style 'Rambo' type which the Prosecution contended had been brought to the scene

1 [2017] EWCA Crim 740

2 https://www.bailii.org/ew/cases/EWCA/Crim/2017/740.html

by Lansana in his bag although it was common ground that the positioning of the CCTV was not such as to identify where the knife came from. The knife was recovered and forensically tested. One swab of blood matched the deceased along with DNA on the handle. Following arrest, Lansana made no comment in interview. Agera, initially made no comment before providing a prepared statement asserting alibi.

At trial, the two defendants asserted that the deceased was in possession of the knife and had produced it after being racially abusive to the third person with them, Guimaraes. An altercation had then taken place during which the knife was dropped and picked up by Agera who stabbed the deceased in self defence. Agera had subsequently wiped it down and disposed of it. Lansana asserted that he had made no physical contact whatsoever with the deceased. Both denied any intention to rob or any robbery. Guimares gave a very different account, describing getting out of the car, seeing the other two go to the back of the car, and Agera say "Let's get it" (which the Prosecution contended was a reference to the knife). They then caught up with the two men and attacked them. One of his co-accused had a knife. He denied that the deceased had racially abused him and said that the victims had done nothing to encourage any aggression.

The case was put on the basis that Agera was the 'stabber'. With regard to Lansana, the jury were directed in accordance with the position pre-*Jogee* and as set out in *Powell and English.* Lansana appealed. Thus, in the case of Lansana, to convict, the jury had to be sure that:

i. Agera was guilty of murder;

ii. he was involved in a joint enterprise to rob;

iii. at the time of embarking on the robbery, he was either carrying a knife or was aware that one of his co-defendants was carrying a knife; and

iv. he realised that there was a real risk that one of his co-defendants might use the knife to stab with the intention of killing or causing really serious bodily harm; and

v. he went ahead and played a part in the robbery in this knowledge.

Lansana asserted that crime A here was the burglary and sought to distinguish the facts from those discussed in Johnson on the basis that the joint enterprise was very much on the spur of the moment: this was not a case of pre-planned use of violence of any sort, let alone such violence involving the knife.

The Court rejected the arguments. Crime A here was one of robbery and the jury had concluded that the joint venture included the use of what was a particularly lethal weapon. It noted the dicta of Lord Hughes and Lord Toulsonin in *Jogee*[3] considering the impact of knowledge of a weapon. Further, once the jury concluded that Lansana knew that Agera might use the knife to stab (i.e. he had that conditional intent), its size could only lead the jury to conclude that he intended that, if used, at least serious bodily injury would be caused. As such there was no substantial injustice. Leave was refused.

The case of *Varley*[4]

Varley was convicted of two counts of robbery and murder relating to the deceased. The deceased lived alone in a flat in Leeds. He was considered vulnerable with both mental and physical difficulties. He had fallen prey to individuals seeking to exploit him for money. Varley was known to him as an alcoholic and drug user. He was not a friend but would visit the deceased uninvited.

---

3 At Para 81.

4 [2017] EWCA Crim 268.

The first robbery took place on 28 January 2015, when Varley and a co-accused, Gath arrived at the deceased's flat and banged on the door, claiming to be police. They had taken steps to conceal their identity from the CCTV and were forensically aware. The deceased called 999 but was told by the operator to open the door to see who it was. Upon doing so the two entered the flat. The deceased was clearly frightened. The call ended abruptly as Gath snatched the phone. Gath then took Mr Gordon's television set off its stand, as Varley threatened to take the television unless the deceased gave them money. Money was handed over and the deceased told Gath where he kept his money. The two men then took £100. Before leaving, Varley punched the deceased on the left cheek, causing a bruise.

The two men returned on 9 February 2015 and were again captured on CCTV taking steps to conceal their identities. They remained in the deceased's flat for approximately 45 minutes. During that time, a friend of the deceased's visited. She knocked on the door in a way that he would have recognised. When the two men left the flat, Varley was seen wearing gloves with his hood up. Gath was seen with a bag containing items taken from the flat including a new replacement television.

The deceased was discovered two days later. The front door was closed but unlocked and the flat had been the subject of an untidy search. It was apparent that a struggle had taken place and it appeared that the deceased had tried to defend himself with a screwdriver. The deceased's body was in the bath covered in blood. An attempt had been made to gag him and he had been smothered in the bath. Water had been poured or showered over his body. DNA linked Gath to the gag. Nothing was found forensically to link Varley with the attack.

Pathology found facial injuries and signs of asphyxia. In addition there were muscle tears and deep bruising across the body, indicative of blunt force trauma, along with gapping fractures in two areas of the spine, associated extensive bleeding and bruising. The latter would have required severe force in order to cause the injury and caused extreme pain. Death was caused by multiple injuries, including severe brain injury. The brain injury was typical of an injury seen in the victim of a car crash, or in somebody who had fallen from a high building. The assault was plainly a brutal one.

Varley gave various accounts in interview, essentially denying being present. This was to change at trial, where he accepted that he took advantage of the deceased but that he visited him to play cards or have a drink. He had gone to the address on 28 January to borrow money. Gath had gone with him for a walk. He denied banging on the door or any robbery. He had asked the deceased for £20-£30 and been given it. The deceased had told Gath where the money was and Gath had taken around £65. He denied threatening or punching Mr Gordon at any stage. He did not know how Mr Gordon had received the bruise to his face.

On the day of the murder, he had visited the flat again but that Gath was solely responsible for the violence inflicted. They had looked for money in the hall cupboard. Gath had hit the deceased. Varley had continued to search the bedroom which is where he had found gloves and put them on. Gath had taken the deceased to the bathroom and shut the door. He did not see or hear any violence. Throughout the 45 minutes in the flat he had spent the time searching for money. He denied taking the bank book, found on the bathroom floor, into the bathroom to question the deceased about the whereabouts of his withdrawals. He could not account for the items strewn around the flat. He believed the deceased was still alive when they left. He agreed that anyone who saw the injuries being inflicted on Mr Gordon would have realised that the intention was to cause really serious harm. He said that if he had become aware of what was happening, he would have tried to stop it. It was Gath who had used all the violence and Gath who had stolen all the property.

Evidence of previous convictions for violence and the fact of four complaints made by the deceased against Varley were before the jury.

The case was left to the jury on the basis of parasitic accessorial liability on the law as understood pre-*Jogee*. At no stage were the jury directed to consider the possibility of a shared intention, or an intention to assist or encourage the principal in the commission of the offence of murder.

The submission on appeal that crime A fell to the lower end of the Johnson spectrum was rejected, instead the Court found it to fall 'towards the upper end of the spectrum'. Whilst the offence of robbery did not involve a weapon, it was a serious crime of violence. The jury were satisfied that they had committed the first robbery and then returned to rob for a second time. The attack on the deceased had begun very soon after entering and Varley must have been aware at the very least of the severity of the assault, being in close proximity on a small flat. He had nonetheless stayed for 45 minutes. Someone had also taken the bank book into the bathroom in an effort to extract information.

In analysing the facts, the Court considered the case through the prism of conditional intent, relying on paragraph 92 of *Jogee*. In those circumstances, the Court held that the only proper inference is that the appellant participated in the robbery with the requisite intent as set out in *Jogee*. The change in the law would not have made a difference and as such the test of substantial injustice had not been made out.

Knowledge of weapons, fundamental difference and supervening act

Whilst withdrawal remains open to a defendant as a defence, *Jogee* has essentially removed the concept of 'fundamental difference'. *Jogee* however inserted a new defence in circumstances where 'some overwhelming supervening act by the perpetrator which nobody in the defendant's shoes could have contemplated might happen and is of such a character as to relegate his acts to history'[5]. As of yet, there has been no guidance as to what may amount to such an act.

5 *Jogee*, at para 81.

The case of *Tas*[6]

Tas examined a line of authorities considering knowledge or otherwise of a weapon and 'fundamental difference' which included *Smith (Wesley)*[7], *Betty*[8] , *Anderson, Morris*[9] , *Reid (Barry)*[10], and *Jogee.*

Tas concerned a conviction for manslaughter. At trial, it was submitted on behalf of Tas that, in his case, the judge should direct the jury that if they were not satisfied that he knew that a knife was being carried by a co-defendant and used by him, then he could not be guilty of manslaughter even if he intended to cause the deceased some harm falling short of really serious harm if the need arose. It was argued that if a knife was being hidden and was then used in what was to have been a fist fight (for example) that could constitute a supervening event (such as would entitle Tas to be acquitted). The prosecution submitted if a defendant takes part in a joint enterprise to do some harm to their victim and the victim dies as a result of the use of a weapon which he did not know was being carried or was to be used in the attack, he was nevertheless guilty of manslaughter. The trial Judge ruled in favour of the Prosecution.

This was appealed on the basis that the judge was wrong to withdraw the possibility of an overwhelming supervening event from the jury.

The Court of Appeal considered the observations in *Jogee*, noting[11] of the judgement that:

6 [2018] EWCA Crim 2603.

7 [1963] 1 WLR 1200.

8 48 Cr App R 6.

9 [1966] 2 QB 110.

10 62 Cr App R 109.

11 At paras 37-38.

> *[I]n underlining the requirement for proof of intention, one of the effects of Jogee is to reduce the significance of knowledge of the weapon so that it impacts as evidence (albeit very important if not potentially irresistible) going to proof of intention, rather than being a pre-requisite of liability for murder. We do not accept that if there is no necessary requirement that the secondary party knows of the weapon in order to bring home a charge of murder (as is the effect of Jogee), the requirement of knowledge of the weapon is reintroduced through the concept of supervening overwhelming event for manslaughter.*
>
> *The argument can be tested in this way. The joint enterprise is to participate in the attack on another and events proceed as happened in this case with Tas punching one of the victims (otherwise than in self-defence), then providing backup (and an escape vehicle) to the others as they chased after them. One of the principals kicks the deceased to death (or, as articulated in [96] of Jogee, the violence has escalated). Alternatively, a bottle is used or a weapon found on the ground. Both based on principle and the correct application of Church (participation by encouragement or assistance in any other unlawful act which all sober and reasonable people would realise carried the risk of some, not necessarily serious, harm to another, with death resulting), a conviction for manslaughter would result: the unlawful act is the intentional use of force otherwise than in self defence.*

The judgment goes on specifically to deal with overwhelming supervening event[12]:

> *40. What then is left of overwhelming supervening act? It is important not to abbreviate the test articulated above which postulates an act that "nobody in the defendant's shoes could have contemplated might happen and is of such a character as to relegate his acts to history". In the context of this case, the question can be*

---

12 At paras 40-41.

asked whether the judge was entitled to conclude that there was insufficient evidence to leave to the jury that if they concluded (as they must have) that, in the course of a confrontation sought by Tas and his friends leading to an ongoing and moving street fight (which had Tas driving his car following the chase to ensure that his friends could be taken from the scene), the production of a knife is a wholly supervening event rather than a simple escalation.

We repeat that in the light of the relegation of knowledge of the weapon as going to proof of intent, it cannot be that the law brings back that knowledge as a pre-requisite for manslaughter. In our judgment, whether there is an evidential basis for overwhelming supervening event which is of such a character as could relegate into history matters which would otherwise be looked on as causative (or, indeed, withdrawal from a joint enterprise) rather than mere escalation which remained part of the joint enterprise is very much for the judge who has heard the evidence and is in a far better position than this court to reach a conclusion as to evidential sufficiency.

As such, the focus is upon the intention of the defendant and not knowledge or otherwise of a weapon. The principle of an overwhelming supervening act was preserved in *Jogee* and remains; however in practice it will be of more limited assistance and confined to a narrower category of case.

One of the primary consequences of *Jogee* has been to broaden the scope for liability in cases where an individual may for example, anticipate a fist fight with an intention to cause really serious harm (e.g. broken bones) which would not have been causative of death but where a fatal injury is inflicted through use of an unknown weapon. Previously, the general direction as often contained in the route to verdict on knowledge of a weapon would have provided a more restrictive route to conviction.

The case of *Harper*[13]

Harper also concerned a challenge to the trial Judge's failure to direct the jury in relation to the potential significance of her ignorance of the knife used in the fatal attack. It was contended that the use of a knife by the co-accused constituted an 'overwhelming supervening act by the perpetrator'. The jury were directed in the following terms:

> *It is Ms Harper's case that she was unaware that Mr Cahill had a knife at the material time. Knowledge or ignorance that Mr Cahill had a particular weapon at the material time will constitute evidence relevant to your determination of whether you can be sure Ms Harper intentionally encouraged and/or assisted Brian Cahill to assault Owen Kerry unlawfully with intent either to kill Mr Kerry or to cause him really serious bodily injury.*

In this regard it was submitted that this was a case in which spontaneous violence erupted and knowledge of a knife was central to the question of Harper's intent. As such the jury ought to have been directed that they had to be sure Harper was aware of the knife. These submissions were said to rely upon observations in *Jogee*.

Unsurprisingly, these submissions were rejected on the basis that it ignored the primary thrust of *Jogee*, which was concerned not with knowledge of weapons but intent.

> *First, intention to assist in a crime of violence is not determined only by whether D2 knows what kind of weapon D1 has in his possession: see Jogee at [98] which goes on:*
>
> > *Knowledge or ignorance that weapons generally or a particular weapon is carried by D1 will be evidence going to what the intention of D2 was, and may be*

13 [2019] EWCA Crim 343.

> *irresistible evidence one way or the other, but it is evidence and no more.*

> *This feature was underlined in R v Brown [2017] EWCA 1870 which makes it clear (at [28]) that knowledge of a weapon used by a principal to inflict harm is not determinative of secondary party liability but is evidence that may inform the jury's decision both as to the intention to cause harm and the level of such harm.*

A concession was made by the Prosecution at sentence as to the fact that it could not be determined whether Harper knew about the weapon was considered to be irrelevant, as 'would be the Judges conclusions as to knowledge' (drawing on the Court's conclusions on the propriety of considering judicial sentencing remarks as part of factual basis for conviction[14]).

The presence of a knife was not an overwhelming supervening event; if that were the case the observations in *Jogee* that such presence was no more than evidence from which the jury could reach conclusions about intention would be wrong. In so finding, the Court drew on the reasoning in *Tas*. In short, if the argument was accepted, it would reverse the development in the law identified by *Jogee.*

CCRC Referrals

It will be noted that to date, there have been only three CCRC referrals to the Court of Appeal following the change of law in *Jogee: Towers*[15], *Daley*[16] *and Mitchell*[17]. None have been successful.

---

14 See, *Johnson* at para 22.

15 [2019] EWCA Crim 198

16 [2019] EWCA Crim 627.

17 *Mitchell (Laura)* (Unreported, 14 November 2018)

At the time of the judgment, the CCRC in a press release noted that:

> *[T]he specific nature of the judgment in Jogee means that the decision will affect other cases only in certain very specific circumstances. The number of cases that end up back at the Court of Appeal will very much depend on matters such as how the individual circumstances of cases relate to the facts in Jogee and on how the attitude of the Court of Appeal develops in relation to Jogee-type cases.*[18]

The approach of the Court of Appeal has been a restrictive one and this is reflected both within *Johnson*, the first set of conjoined appeals and those that have followed. The fact that there have been only three referrals may therefore be disappointing however it is not surprising.

There has been an attempt to judicially review the approach of the CCRC: *R (on the application of Davies) v CCRC*[19] discussed further below. First, it is worth considering the three referrals themselves.

The case of *Mitchell*

Mitchell was the first of the CCRC referrals. Of note, Mitchell was a co-defendant of Hall, one of the conjoined appeals and unsuccessful applicants considered in *Johnson*.

In 2007, Mitchell along with Hall and Henry Ballantyne were convicted of the murder of Andrew Ayres and violent disorder. In the early hours of Sunday 28 January 2007 a dispute arose over a taxi. A group had booked a taxi; however upon its arrival Mitchell along with the others had got in. The taxi driver realised that they were not his fare and asked them to get out. At the same time one of the original group

18 Criminal Cases Review Commission, (2016) *The CCRC, "joint enterprise" and the judgment in the case of Ameen Jogee.*, available at <https://ccrc.gov.uk/the-ccrc-joint-enterprise-and-the-judgment-in-the-case-of-ameen-jogee/>.

19 [2018] EWHC 3080 (Admin).

who had booked the taxi came out of the pub and asked them to get out. All had consumed substantial amounts of alcohol. At this stage, Mitchell was reported to have become aggressive and began to argue with a female in the other group. Initially others tried to calm her down before they also became violent. Kicking and punching took place. At this stage two others including the deceased came out of the pub and became involved. The first pulled one of the attackers (most likely Hall) away and Mitchell jumped onto his back. He shrugged her off but was then attacked with kicks and punches by the co-accused. The evidence of an independent witness was that Mitchell was part of a determined attempt to get two males to the ground and were kicking and punching them. It was the prosecution case that the only conceivable purpose was to kick them whilst they were on the ground. There was then a lull in the violence.

During this period Mitchell was looking for her shoes which had come off in the incident. At least two co-accused, not including Mitchell or Hall, went to a nearby house and returned to the car park with a mace, CS gas and a knuckleduster. The deceased and the two earlier victims of the assault walked to the mouth of the road where the co-accused had gone. At that point the deceased was uninjured. Anticipating that they were to be attacked, they retraced their steps to the pub. But found themselves locked out. A number of the co-accused, returned to the car park. The deceased's group were sprayed with CS gas and chased. One escaped, the second was caught by three attackers, including Hall and attacked in the car park (pulled to the ground, punched and kicked).

The deceased was also caught by the group in the car park, knocked to the floor and set upon. Carl Holmes stamped on his head and upper neck brutally and repeatedly, causing injuries from which he subsequently died in hospital. His injuries were caused by shod feet and not any other weapon. There was no evidence that it was anyone other than Holmes who was engaged in stamping on the deceased's head. There were no injuries to his legs, other than scuff abrasions over the right knee. There were no marks of any significance to the back or chest other than a mark in the region of the left nipple.

There was, however, evidence that a group were involved in the attack. Some were kicking and hitting a person on the floor and the head of that person was then stamped on; however the accounts varied and the evidence that the person on the floor was being kicked by others was not consistent with the pathology. The whole incident therefore only lasted a few minutes.

After the deceased had been attacked, the fighting stopped. Hall and Mitchell went to the nearby house from where they left by taxi shortly afterwards. It was Mitchell's case that she had been looking for her shoes throughout the second incident.

Although there had been a short lull in the violence, it was the prosecution case that there was one single joint enterprise in which there was a common intent to cause serious bodily injury through the use of shod feet or other weapons to the two men and the deceased so as to teach them a lesson because they had dared to stand up to them. There were two alternative bases for conviction, shared intention or on principles of secondary liability (foresight).

The Court held that Mitchell had started the initial violence. It was open to the jury to infer that she had the necessary (conditional) intent "arguably from the outset". In her case evidence of foresight (which must have been at a minimum found by the jury) was strong evidence of her intention. Withdrawal from the joint venture was rejected. There had been no communication of any withdrawal.

Conditional intent featured prominently within the Court's consideration; however it was not discussed in any significant detail within the judgment and the analysis of the facts on the Court's view appears to have been more aligned with an ongoing intention, rather than conditional intention.

The Court, as in *Towers* (below) reiterated the high hurdle and threshold presented by the "substantial injustice" test and noted its power in section 16C of the Criminal Appeal Act 1968 to dismiss referrals from the CCRC summarily if based on a change of law. It may be that this serves as a warning from the Court to the CCRC.

The case of *Towers*[20]

Towers was a CCRC referral to the Court of Appeal on the basis of a pre I direction based on parasitic accessorial liability. This followed an earlier unsuccessful application for leave to appeal conviction in 2008 which was predicated on different grounds. In 2007, Jordan Towers was convicted of murder and wounding with intent contrary to s. 18 of the Offences Against the Person Act 1861, alongside Anthony Stewart Hawkes and Dean Curtis. Towers and Hawkes were both aged under 18 at the date of the offence.

The CCRC referred the murder conviction of Towers (but not that for wounding with intent) on the basis of the change of law brought about by *Jogee* and the clarification given in *Johnson.*

In May 2007, Kevin Johnson was fatally stabbed outside his home in Sunderland. This followed an altercation with three young men who had been behaving rowdily in the street, Towers (then aged 16), Hawkes (then aged 17) and Curtis (then aged 19). The fatal wound was inflicted by either Hawkes or Curtis. In a second incident five minutes later, another male encountered the same three on a nearby street and was stabbed in the chest by Hawkes. The injury was not life-threatening but required hospital treatment and two stitches. This was the offence of wounding with intent contrary to s.18 OAPA.

It was not in dispute that all three were in possession of weapons. Towers admitted to the police that he had been carrying a knife and that he had discarded it later during the evening after the incident. He led police to where he had left it. The knife was subsequently excluded as the murder weapon (which was never found). No blood was found

20 [2019] EWCA Crim 198.

on his clothing. Hawkes admitted that he had been carrying a Stanley knife and Curtis admitted carrying a screwdriver.

Towers accepted that he had thrown some punches at the deceased and had picked up a broken paving slab (also described as a rock or brick) and thrown it at him but none had connected. However he denied participation in the stabbing (which appears to have occurred before the slab was thrown). In relation to the latter attack, it was contended that there was no evidence of him being involved in any abuse, threat or attack, or even encouragement.

The prosecution case was advanced on the basis that murder would be established if the fatal injury was inflicted with each of the three intending to cause the deceased really serious harm or, alternatively, on the basis that they had foresight that serious bodily injury could be inflicted. In contrast, the count of wounding with intent was put only on the basis of a shared intent.

In considering the appeal, the Court considered the evidence in detail.

The deceased's partner saw three males, two of whom were attacking and the third of which (Towers) who was in the middle of the street some 15-20 feet away. Another eye witness described a similar scene but with the third boy 'enticing' the deceased to come around the corner towards him and two others. All three were said to surround and close in on the deceased. The second boy was in front of the deceased and made a motion with his left hand three times. The third boy (Towers) stayed some four feet away. The other two continued to strike the deceased. The third boy then picked up a paving slab, held it at head height and threw it at the deceased; it was unclear whether the slab missed or struck him on the legs. This third boy (said to be Towers) went further into the road, away from the other two, then back towards them. By the time the deceased's partner had come outside the three were walking away, laughing. The third male was at all times further from the deceased than the others, who were "taking the lead". The deceased had been stabbed four times.

There was some evidence of a dispute arising between the three boys, with a third catching up with the other two and potentially initiating an argument over something that had been done and which at least two of the boys were unhappy about and asking about. The second stabbing then took place, and was followed by a further incident in the early hours of the morning at a Shell petrol station. Two of the three (said to be Hawkes and Curtis) were aggressive and threatening. The third (Towers) stood away from them and after the threats asked for some crisps, proffering a £1 coin. The other two then threw a brick at a window which cracked.

The Prosecution relied on evidence from Towers' mother and sister about his reaction that evening and adduced a conversation between him and Curtis. Towers had denied involvement and told his sister that the other two were responsible.

Towers declined to give evidence at trial. The accounts in interview were before the jury. Hawkes and Curtis gave evidence blaming each other but exculpating Towers.

The route to verdict posited both shared intent (question 7) or the alternative based on foresight in accordance with the law as set out in *Powell and English*:

> *(5) Having concluded that this Defendant did not inflict the fatal stab wound, are you sure that he joined in unlawfully in the attack on [the deceased] before the fatal stab wound was inflicted? If your answer to that is yes, you go on to question 6. If your answer to that question is no, the Defendant is not guilty of murder and not guilty of manslaughter.*
>
> *(6) Are you sure that this Defendant knew that the perpetrator had a knife? If you are sure of that, you go to question 7. If you are not sure, that Defendant is not guilty of murder or manslaughter.*

(7) Are you sure that this Defendant shared the perpetrator's intention either to kill or cause really serious bodily harm with the knife? If your answer to that question is yes, he is guilty of murder. If your answer to that question is no, you go to question 8.

(8) Are you sure that this Defendant realised that the perpetrator might use the knife with an intention either to kill or cause really serious bodily harm, but nevertheless took part in the attack?

If your answer to that is yes, that Defendant is guilty of murder. If your answer to that question is no, then that defendant is not guilty of either murder or manslaughter. But that Defendant would be guilty of manslaughter if you were sure that he participated in the attack and that he realised that the perpetrator might use the knife with the intention of causing some harm, not serious harm, but some harm which is short of really serious bodily harm."

The CCRC conducted an analysis of the evidence. It is instructive to consider the conclusions and approach of the CCRC:

i. The principal intentionally inflicted really serious harm on Johnson, and not acting in self-defence;

ii. Towers joined unlawfully in the attack before the fatal wound was inflicted;

iii. Towers knew the principal had a knife; and

iv. He either shared the principal's intention to kill or cause really serious harm, or realised that the principal might use the knife with an intention to kill or cause really serious harm and nevertheless took part in the attack.

This could be distinguished from the s18 OAPA offence, where albeit there was a lack of clarity in the language of the route to verdict, when the totality of the summing up was considered Towers could only have been convicted of wounding with intent if the jury concluded that he shared Hawkes' intention to inflict grievous bodily harm.

The CCRC then considered the (largely undisputed) facts that could be drawn:

i. Towers was part of the group that provoked a fight with Mr Johnson;

ii. On his own admission he was drunk and threw some early punches and a paving slab;

iii. The paving slab was thrown towards Johnson, though it was unclear whether it hit him and whether it was before or after the fatal injury was inflicted;

iv. Towers was standing off during the struggle in which Johnson was stabbed;

v. The stabbing of Johnson had been unexpected or unwelcome to at least one person in the party;

vi. All the defendants had weapons;

vii. Towers had stopped Thompson in the street and engaged with him, intending (with Hawkes and Curtis) that he be caused really serious harm; and

viii. Towers remained in the group for some hours after the first two incidents and was with them during the third.

The CCRC then moved to consider the likelihood that a direction based on the new law would have made a difference at trial. It concluded that the argument that the change in the law would have led to a different verdict was sufficiently strong to refer the case, relying on seven evidential arguments which, in its view, 'significantly weakened' the safety of the inference of requisite intention on the part of Towers. These were:

i. The attack on the deceased was an unplanned outbreak of disorder/violence caused by a chance encounter rather than part of a prior criminal venture where associated serious violence, 'if necessary' or 'if it came to it', was inherently likely;

ii. The joint enterprise from which it arose was 'nebulous' and may not have amounted to more than a general intention to be 'looking for trouble' or to engage in a fight, albeit while carrying weapons.

iii. Towers' own actions amounted merely to involvement in an unarmed scuffle and drunkenly throwing a brick; at the time of the fatal attack he was standing away, watching;

iv. 'Given the nature of the evidence against Mr Towers and the facts of the case' it is likely that foresight rather than personal or shared intention to commit really serious harm was central to his conviction;

v. In the view of the CCRC, 'none' of the evidence which established Towers' participation in the incident, suggested an intention to encourage or assist others to use their weapons against the deceased;

vi. The later evidence suggested that either Towers or a second member of the party was angry with the principal and challenged him about what happened. If it was Towers, it was good evidence that he did not have the requisite intention. If it was another of the pair who fought the deceased, 'it speaks even more to how unexpectedly the knife had in fact been produced and used by the principal' (emphasis from the CCRC);

vii. The incident at the Shell petrol station demonstrated that Towers stayed with the others while they committed very serious offences and had a high tolerance of their behaviour, but 'did not appear to commit or encourage any offences himself'. There was 'no inevitable connection between his association and any involvement in committing or encouraging any criminal conduct'.

Further, the CCRC considered that the fact that Towers was himself carrying a knife could not be taken as evidence of either a generalised intention to commit really serious harm or intention to encourage really serious harm in the 'highly unusual circumstances', which included the lack of production, telling the police about it and his explanation. Similarly, the conviction for the later count of wounding with intent did not preclude referral where the CCRC considered that the arguments on the murder count were strong and that the intention found in the latter incident could not be read across.

The CCRC concluded that as required by *Johnson*, there was a real possibility that the Court would find that this was a case involving a 'substantial injustice'. In doing so it noted that Towers would inevitably be guilty of manslaughter and ancillary offences; however considered the unique stigma of a conviction for murder, Towers' youth and the approach of the Court in *Ordu*[21] to countervail.

The Court rejected these contentions. The starting point was that Towers was involved in a joint enterprise to use unlawful force on the victim with the knowledge that both he and the principals had weapons. He foresaw the possibility that really serious harm would be caused to the victim. A number of features were, in the court's view, determinative:

21 [2017] EWCA Crim 4

i. Towers involved himself in a joint enterprise knowing that he and the others were armed;

ii. He took part in, or associated himself with, the attack by lifting and throwing a paving slab at the first victim when two others were or had been attacking him;

iii. He went on, with the intention of causing grievous bodily harm, to involve himself in the attack (whether by attracting his attention, encouraging or otherwise): the fact that the defendant might have had animus to one of the victims did not undermine the intention found by the jury to have been proved in an attack so soon after that the victim who was killed.

The Court noted[22] that:

> *[F]ollowing Johnson, in circumstances in which 'crime A' was itself a crime of violence where the principal was known to be armed combined with involvement, very shortly thereafter, in a further attack with a proved intention to cause grievous bodily harm, we are satisfied that Towers has not been the victim of a substantial injustice as a result of the change in the law.*

The submission that owing to his youth, Towers was 'susceptible to peer pressure and had an adolescent concern to avoid exclusion' was rejected on the basis that there was 'absolutely no evidence from Towers to that effect' – Towers not having given evidence at trial. To date, and as discussed further when considering *Grant-Murray & Ors*, there has been no adjustment or difference in approach to cases involving youth, immaturity and in particular child defendants.

Significant argument also concerned the test of substantial injustice. The Court emphatically rejected the submission that the test was similar to that applied when assessing the safety of the conviction. The

22 At para 72.

test was distinct, carrying with it a considerably higher threshold for substantial injustice so as to justify interference with the conviction.

The case of *Daley*[23]

Daley was convicted of the murder of Umar Tufail. It was the Prosecution's case that Daley was the front seat passenger in a car driven by his co-accused Thomas. The deceased was sitting in a car outside his home, when the car driven by Thomas pulled up alongside and fired a single shot through its open passenger window, striking the deceased in the head and causing the fatal injury. Expert evidence was of little assistance in determining the position of the shooter within the car. The two accused remained together after the incident and continued to communicate and meet up. Daley disposed of his phones, clothing and footwear. He resigned from his job and there was evidence of a partially completed application for a passport.

The Prosecution alleged that there was a gang background to the offending. The deceased's brother had previously stabbed the co-accused. The shooting was an execution, a deliberate shot fired at almost point blank range, carried out in furtherance of an ongoing dispute between two rival gangs. Whoever was the gunman both men in the car were fully involved in the criminal enterprise to shoot and kill.

At trial Daley admitted that his co-accused had shot the victim, but he denied any prior knowledge of the gun or the intention of his co-accused. The co-accused sought to assert that a third person was in the car and had fired the shot; however this was undermined by CCTV and forensic evidence.

23 [2019] EWCA Crim 627.

Daley initially appealed his conviction, raising issues connected to PAL. This was dismissed and following *Jogee*, he made an application to the CCRC.

The CCRC referred the matter back to the Court of Appeal on the basis that it was likely that he had been convicted on foresight only and that applying *Johnson* the change of the law would have made a difference to the outcome of his trial.

This was rejected by the Court who held on the basis of the jury directions and route to verdict that:

i. Daley and the co-accused were in a joint enterprise to possess a loaded gun;

ii. Daley encouraged or assisted in that offence;

iii. Daley realised that the gun might be used to commit murder;

iv. His knowledge of the gun gave rise to a very strong inference of participation with intent to cause really serious harm;

v. As such there was no substantial injustice as Daley could not demonstrate that a *Jogee* compliant direction would have made a difference to the verdict.

As seen in other cases, knowledge of the weapon, here a firearm was ultimately fatal to the appeal, considered as it is, as strong evidence of intent (as per *Johnson*)

The approach of the CCRC

In 2018, a judicial review challenge was brought to the CCRC's refusal to refer the Claimant's pre-Jogee conviction for murder to the Court of Appeal: *R (on the application of Davies) v CCRC.*[24] The judgment is instructive in considering the CCRC's approach to the review of historic cases potentially engaging *Jogee* and substantial injustice, the relationship to assessing whether there is a "real possibility" that the conviction would not be upheld, the analytical framework employed and the approach of the Court to decisions of the CCRC.

In brief, the Claimant was convicted of the murder of Edward Simpson, who was battered to death during the course of a robbery at his home. The Claimant was not present, but was an active organiser of the crime and was convicted on the basis of joint enterprise principles. The jury was directed in accordance within the then understanding of the law, namely that it was sufficient that a defendant was party to the joint enterprise, in this case the robbery, and foresaw that as part of that joint enterprise serious injury might be inflicted. There was no dispute that the Claimant was a party to the robbery (it concerning a substantial sum of money and drugs), being fully involved in setting it up and the recruitment of other men to conduct it.

The robbers took an imitation firearm and a large adjustable wrench to the scene. The deceased was beaten with the wrench, causing multiple very severe, and in due course fatal, injuries. However, he did not die immediately. The violence used was extreme, taking place in a number of locations within the property and also including suffocation, ligatures and the pouring of water over the deceased's head whilst inside a pillowcase. Another man arrived at the property during the robbery and was also seriously assaulted to the head and threatened with the imitation firearm. The deceased was later taken from the property while badly injured but still alive. There was some evidence, hotly contested, that the Claimant had received a phone call at this stage and was

24 [2018] EWHC 3080 (Admin).

'endorsing' the violence used and expressing no surprise. This was said to go to the issue of foresight and intent. The deceased was found dead some hours later in the grounds of a deserted nursing home. Evidence of previous violent attacks by the Claimant and others (unproven) were adduced by the Prosecution.

In a provisional decision of 20 March 2017, followed by a final decision on 29 September 2017, the CCRC declined to refer the matter.

The Claimant submitted that the CCRC had misdirected itself by permitting the remarks of the CACD in *Johnson* and the substantial injustice test to 'divert' it from the statutory test (one of 'real possibility') when the statutory test remained the necessary approach of the CCRC. The CCRC accepted that there had been a material misdirection; however it was correct to consider the substantial injustice test. That was intrinsic to and required by the statutory test: in addressing whether there was a 'real possibility' that the Court would quash this conviction, the Commission was bound to take into account the approach the Court would adopt to such an appeal.

The Court held[25]:

> *Since [the CCRC's] task is to predict a real possibility of a successful appeal, they are bound to do so from the starting point of examining the legal approach which will be taken by the Court to the case in hand. Hence, the requirement that there should be demonstrated that 'substantial injustice' before such an appeal should be permitted to progress, was bound to be incorporated into the thinking of the Commission. Implicit in some of the submissions from [the claimant] was the idea that Johnson was wrongly decided, with the result that the 'high threshold' was too high. The need for 'substantial injustice' has been laid down in long-standing authority, and has been explicitly approved by the Supreme Court in Jogee and the Court of Appeal in*

25 At paras 59-60.

> *Johnson. It can be no part of the role of the Commission to take a different view, and proceed as if that test was misguided.*
>
> *In my view the decision in Crilly adds nothing to the approach here ... the Court of Appeal expressly confirmed the ratio laid down in Johnson. Crilly does not represent any 'developing' of the law, merely an application of the established approach to particular facts...*

In considering the merits and safety, the Court held that there was a very strong case on the facts of conditional intent and that the conviction was far from unsafe.

Principles to be distilled

The *Johnson* spectrum

The spectrum of crime A and crime B as identified in *Johnson* appears to be of limited assistance and problematic when considering cases of escalating or spontaneous violence and where there is more than one precursor offences. For example where a burglary becomes a robbery and then results in the murder of the homeowner. Which is crime A - the burglary or the robbery? Similarly, where the initial offence is one of lower level violence or causing trouble but then escalates. There have been differing approaches to the issue by the Court. If the offence does not fall towards the lower end, it appears unlikely that the Court will interfere. It has been suggested that a far better approach is to approach it by asking which offence(s) the secondary party intentionally assisted or encouraged.

Knowledge or possession of a weapon

It appears increasingly unlikely that any appeal concerning a situation in which the Applicant was either armed or aware that others were armed will succeed. There is an irony present when it is considered that knowledge of a knife was not considered to be determinative for fixing criminal liability in *Jogee*; however is essentially determinative of whether an applicant can demonstrate substantial injustice.

Conditional intent

There is an increasing approach by the Court of Appeal to infer conditional intent from evidence of foresight. It is in the authors' experience the general submission made in the Form RN by the Prosecution. This is particularly difficult to counter in cases of spontaneous and escalating violence. The concept is not however without its difficulties and as of yet has not been fully explored or considered by the Court. In short, conditional intent is nonetheless intent. In such circumstances, the Court should be wary of falling into the same trap as that prior to the change of law with evidence of foresight equating to authorization as regards conditional intent.

Substitution of the court's analysis of the facts

It is arguable that in some of the cases which have come before the Court, it has impermissibly substituted its version of the facts in place of that of the jury.[26] Questions remain for example as to what is the relevance of a majority verdict finding guilt on the sole basis of foresight, the lower basis for guilt.

Substantial injustice and safety

Following on from *Johnson*, the Court of Appeal has confirmed that the threshold for substantial injustice is significantly higher and distinct from that of the safety of the conviction: in essence whether the change of law in *Jogee* would have made a difference to the conviction. Challenges in this regard have failed. At present, as set out above this test is only likely to be satisfied in cases where the applicant was not in possession of a weapon, was unaware that the principal or other co-accused

---

26 *Pendleton* [2002] 1 Cr App R 34

were carrying weapons and did not set out to commit or participate in offences of violence (or in all likelihood public disorder – affray etc).

CHAPTER SIX
CURRENT APPLICATION OF JOGEE

As has been discussed the impact of *Jogee* on historic cases has been negligible. The more likely impact concerns those cases following the Supreme Court decision and in the future.

In the immediate aftermath of *Jogee* a number of trials were either halted or successful submissions of no case to answer were made on the basis of the change in law.

In such cases the Prosecution has the ability to appeal the decision under the terminatory ruling mechanism[1]. The Court of Appeal considered such a case in *Anwar and Others*[2] approximately a month after the Supreme Court handed down judgment. This was the Court of Appeal's first opportunity to consider the decision in *Jogee.* The Court noted that evidence relied upon previously to infer foresight, was likely to be the same as that now relied on to infer the requisite intent: 'the evidential requirements justifying a decision that there is a case to answer are likely to be the same even if, applying the facts to the different directions in law, the jury might reach a different conclusion'[3]. Thus, the same facts which would previously have been used to support the inference of *mens rea* before the decision in *Jogee* will equally be used now. In demonstrating the relatively limited potential impact the Court observed that '[w]e find it difficult to foresee circumstances in which there might have been a case to answer under the law before *Jogee* but, because of the way in which the law is now articulated, there no longer is'[4].

1 Section 58, Criminal Justice Act 2003.

2 [2016] EWCA Crim 551.

3 [2016] EWCA Crim 551, para 22.

4 [2016] EWCA Crim 551, para 20.

It is difficult to assess the impact on current cases. It is the authors' experience that cases which may previously have been put on the basis of foresight are now being placed before the jury on the basis that either the individuals concerned are joint principals or alternatively, shared the necessary intent. This is not altogether surprising given that in practice, many Judges were already summing up on the basis of an intention to cause at least really serious harm and not foresight prior to the judgment in *Jogee* and the observations in *Anwar*.

The area of greatest impact is perhaps with regard to those individuals on the periphery of the relevant acts and where the jury is considering the murder and manslaughter distinction. In such cases, there has been a greater number of manslaughter convictions and murder acquittals owing to the higher mental element required. It will be interesting to see if manslaughter prosecutions become more common.

Change in CPS guidance

The CPS undertook a consultation on the development of new charging guidance in cases engaging principles of joint enterprise[5]. The guidance covers:

i. The law on secondary liability following the decision in *R v Jogee; Ruddock v The Queen* [2016] UKSC 8; UKPC 7.

ii. The abolition of "parasitic accessory liability" as a basis for criminal liability.

iii. The liability of an accessory based on conditional intent.

iv. The evidential value of association and presence.

5 Director of Public Prosecutions, 'Secondary Liability: charging decisions on principals and accessories', in *The Code for Crown Prosecutors*, available at <https://www.cps.gov.uk/legal-guidance/secondary-liability-charging-decisions-principals-and-accessories>.

v. The evidential value of an accessory's knowledge of weapons.

vi. How to select charges that involve principal, secondary and inchoate liability.

vii. The approach to charging group assaults, including cases of murder and manslaughter.

viii. Charging offences under the Serious Crime Act 2007.

ix. Recording the basis for charging decisions.

International Application

The decision in *Jogee* has aroused significant international interest. It is unusual for a court as well respected as the Supreme Court and Privy Council to admit that it has made a mistake. It is perhaps even more remarkable when it is in such a fundamental principle as how liability attaches for secondary offenders in murder. This section will briefly look at how the decision has been considered in Australia and Hong Kong as well as discussing what impact it may have on the international tribunals.

Australia and Hong Kong have a particular significance for the study of PAL. The seeds of the doctrine can be traced back to the Australian cases of *Johns*[6] and *Miller*[7], while the doctrine itself was finally expounded in terms in an appeal from the Court of Appeal of Hong Kong to the Privy Council.

The Australian experience is in some ways a journey from the case of one appellant called Miller to another. Both *Johns* and *Miller* were not, on their facts, PAL cases at all. In Johns the appellant was a getaway

6 *Johns v The Queen* [1980] HCA 3, (1980) 143 CLR 108.

7 *Miller v The Queen* (1980) 55 ALJR 23.

driver and there was evidence that he had given his assent to the principal to use a gun if necessary. In Miller there was no 'crime A' as picking up women for consensual sex is not a crime. The endeavour only became criminal when the women were killed. In both cases either common purpose liability or simple accessorial liability was sufficient to found liability[8].

It is from these cases that PAL was born in Australia. Post-Jogee it is in another case called *Miller*[9] that the principle was re-confirmed, notwithstanding the fact that the Supreme Court and Privy Council found that it was a mistake in law. In the 2016 case of *Miller* the High Court of Australia found that PAL (which is often referred to as 'extended common purpose' in Australia[10]) continued to be good law in that jurisdiction. This, according to Baker, was based on the policy position of those judges who formed the majority 'rather than solid legal argument'[11]. *Miller* (2016) is the most recent confirmation of the validity of PAL in Australian law after the High Court refused an appeal by finding that PAL was a proper foundation for liability in the 2006 case of *Clayton*[12]. *Miller* thus marks an unusual divergence of the High Court of Australia and the UK Supreme Court on such a fundamental common law principle as the law of complicity in murder[13].

The principles in Chan Wing-Siu were faithfully followed in the courts of Hong Kong and the decision was re-affirmed after the handover of the region to China in the case of *Sze Kwan Lung*[14]. In the late 2016

8 Knowles, J (2016), 'Joint Enterprise After *Jogee and Ruddock*: What Next?', *UK Supreme Court Yearbook,* Vol 7, pp 72-128, at pp 111-113.

9 *Miller v The Queen* [2016] HCA 30.

10 Knowles, J p 87

11 Baker, D (2017) 'Jogee: jury directions and the manslaughter alternative', *Crim LR*, 1, 51-56.

12 *Clayton v The Queen* [2006] HCA 58, (2006) 231 ALR 500.

13 Simester, A (2017) 'Accessory liability and common unlawful purposes', *Law Quarterly Review*, 133 (Jan), 73-90.

case of *Chan Kam-Shing*[15] the Court of Final Appeal of Hong Kong found that there had been no wrong-turn in *Chan Wing-Siu*. This is another case which is not factually a PAL case. The appeal was dismissed on the facts as there was enough evidence to justify conviction on the basis of basic accessorial liability. Like *Miller* it is driven by policy considerations[16] and serves to maintain PAL as a form of liability in Hong Kong.

---

14 *Sze Kwan Lung and others v Hong Kong Special Autonomous Region* [2004] HKCFA 85; [2004] 3 HKLRD 328; (2004) 7 HKCFAR 475; FACC 6/2004. See also Cheung, E (2016) *The Dichotomy Between Foresight and Intention in Joint Enterprise Murder: Should Our Top Court Depart From Chan Wing-Siu and Sze Kwan Lung?*, Centre for Comparative and Public Law Faculty of Law, The University of Hong Kong, Occasional Paper No. 28.

15 *Chan Kam-Shing v Hong Kong Special Autonomous Region* [2016] HKCFA 87; FACC No. 5 of 2016.

16 Krebs, B (2017) 'Hong Kong Court of Final Appeal: Divided by a Common Purpose', *Journal of Criminal Law*, Vol. 81(4) 271–274.

MORE BOOKS BY LAW BRIEF PUBLISHING

A selection of our other titles available now:-

'Ellis on Credit Hire – Sixth Edition' by Aidan Ellis & Tim Kevan
'A Practical Guide to Coercive Control for Legal Practitioners and Victims' by Rachel Horman
'A Practical Guide to Rights Over Airspace and Subsoil' by Daniel Gatty
'Tackling Disclosure in the Criminal Courts – A Practitioner's Guide' by Narita Bahra QC & Don Ramble
'A Practical Guide to the Law of Driverless Cars – Second Edition' by Alex Glassbrook, Emma Northey & Scarlett Milligan
'A Practical Guide to TOLATA Claims' by Greg Williams
'Artificial Intelligence – The Practical Legal Issues' by John Buyers
'A Practical Guide to the Law of Bullying and Harassment in the Workplace' by Philip Hyland
'How to Be a Freelance Solicitor: A Practical Guide to the SRA-Regulated Freelance Solicitor Model' by Paul Bennett
'A Practical Guide to Prison Injury Claims' by Malcolm Johnson
'A Practical Guide to the Small Claims Track' by Dominic Bright
'A Practical Guide to Advising Clients at the Police Station' by Colin Stephen McKeown-Beaumont
'A Practical Guide to Antisocial Behaviour Injunctions' by Iain Wightwick
'Practical Mediation: A Guide for Mediators, Advocates, Advisers, Lawyers, and Students in Civil, Commercial, Business, Property, Workplace, and Employment Cases' by Jonathan Dingle with John Sephton
'The Mini-Pupillage Workbook' by David Boyle
'Planning Obligations Demystified: A Practical Guide to Planning Obligations and Section 106 Agreements' by Bob Mc Geady & Meyric Lewis
'A Practical Guide to Crofting Law' by Brian Inkster

'A Practical Guide to Spousal Maintenance' by Liz Cowell
'A Practical Guide to the Law of Domain Names and Cybersquatting' by Andrew Clemson
'A Practical Guide to the Law of Gender Pay Gap Reporting' by Harini Iyengar
'A Practical Guide to the Rights of Grandparents in Children Proceedings' by Stuart Barlow
'NHS Whistleblowing and the Law' by Joseph England
'Employment Law and the Gig Economy' by Nigel Mackay & Annie Powell
'A Practical Guide to the General Data Protection Regulation (GDPR)' by Keith Markham
'A Practical Guide to Noise Induced Hearing Loss (NIHL) Claims' by Andrew Mckie, Ian Skeate, Gareth McAloon
'An Introduction to Beauty Negligence Claims – A Practical Guide for the Personal Injury Practitioner' by Greg Almond
'Intercompany Agreements for Transfer Pricing Compliance' by Paul Sutton
'Zen and the Art of Mediation' by Martin Plowman
'A Practical Guide to the SRA Principles, Individual and Law Firm Codes of Conduct 2019 – What Every Law Firm Needs to Know' by Paul Bennett
'A Practical Guide to Licensing Law for Commercial Property Lawyers' by Niall McCann & Richard Williams
'A Practical Guide to Adoption for Family Lawyers' by Graham Pegg
'A Practical Guide to Industrial Disease Claims' by Andrew Mckie & Ian Skeate
'A Practical Guide to Redundancy' by Philip Hyland
'A Practical Guide to Vicarious Liability' by Mariel Irvine
'A Practical Guide to Claims Arising from Delays in Diagnosing Cancer' by Bella Webb
'A Practical Guide to Applications for Landlord's Consent and Variation of Leases' by Mark Shelton
'A Practical Guide to Relief from Sanctions Post-Mitchell and Denton' by Peter Causton
'A Practical Guide to Equity Release for Advisors' by Paul Sams
'A Practical Guide to Unlawful Eviction and Harassment' by Stephanie Lovegrove

'A Practical Guide to the Law Relating to Food' by Ian Thomas
'A Practical Guide to the Ending of Assured Shorthold Tenancies' by Elizabeth Dwomoh
'A Practical Guide to Financial Services Claims' by Chris Hegarty
'The Law of Houses in Multiple Occupation: A Practical Guide to HMO Proceedings' by Julian Hunt
'A Practical Guide to Unlawful Eviction and Harassment' by Stephanie Lovegrove
'A Practical Guide to Solicitor and Client Costs' by Robin Dunne
'A Practical Guide to Wrongful Conception, Wrongful Birth and Wrongful Life Claims' by Rebecca Greenstreet
'Occupiers, Highways and Defective Premises Claims: A Practical Guide Post-Jackson – 2nd Edition' by Andrew Mckie
'A Practical Guide to Financial Ombudsman Service Claims' by Adam Temple & Robert Scrivenor
'A Practical Guide to the Law of Enfranchisement and Lease Extension' by Paul Sams
'A Practical Guide to Marketing for Lawyers – 2nd Edition' by Catherine Bailey & Jennet Ingram
'A Practical Guide to Advising Schools on Employment Law' by Jonathan Holden
'Certificates of Lawful Use and Development: A Guide to Making and Determining Applications' by Bob Mc Geady & Meyric Lewis
'A Guide to Consent in Clinical Negligence Post-Montgomery' by Lauren Sutherland QC
'A Practical Guide to Running Housing Disrepair and Cavity Wall Claims: 2nd Edition' by Andrew Mckie & Ian Skeate
'A Practical Guide to Holiday Sickness Claims – 2nd Edition' by Andrew Mckie & Ian Skeate
'Arguments and Tactics for Personal Injury and Clinical Negligence Claims' by Dorian Williams
'A Practical Guide to QOCS and Fundamental Dishonesty' by James Bentley
'A Practical Guide to Drone Law' by Rufus Ballaster, Andrew Firman, Eleanor Clot
'A Practical Guide to Compliance for Personal Injury Firms Working With Claims Management Companies' by Paul Bennett

'A Practical Guide to the Landlord and Tenant Act 1954: Commercial Tenancies' by Richard Hayes & David Sawtell
'A Practical Guide to Dog Law for Owners and Others' by Andrea Pitt
'RTA Allegations of Fraud in a Post-Jackson Era: The Handbook – 2nd Edition' by Andrew Mckie
'RTA Personal Injury Claims: A Practical Guide Post-Jackson' by Andrew Mckie
'On Experts: CPR35 for Lawyers and Experts' by David Boyle
'An Introduction to Personal Injury Law' by David Boyle
'A Practical Guide to Claims Arising From Accidents Abroad and Travel Claims' by Andrew Mckie & Ian Skeate
'A Practical Guide to Chronic Pain Claims' by Pankaj Madan
'A Practical Guide to Claims Arising from Fatal Accidents' by James Patience
'A Practical Approach to Clinical Negligence Post-Jackson' by Geoffrey Simpson-Scott
'Employers' Liability Claims: A Practical Guide Post-Jackson' by Andrew Mckie
'A Practical Guide to Subtle Brain Injury Claims' by Pankaj Madan
'A Practical Guide to Costs in Personal Injury Cases' by Matthew Hoe
'The No Nonsense Solicitors' Practice: A Guide To Running Your Firm' by Bettina Brueggemann
'The Queen's Counsel Lawyer's Omnibus: 20 Years of Cartoons from The Times 1993-2013' by Alex Steuart Williams

These books and more are available to order online direct from the publisher at www.lawbriefpublishing.com, where you can also read free sample chapters. For any queries, contact us on 0844 587 2383 or mail@lawbriefpublishing.com.

Our books are also usually in stock at www.amazon.co.uk with free next day delivery for Prime members, and at good legal bookshops such as Wildy & Sons.

We are regularly launching new books in our series of practical day-to-day practitioners' guides. Visit our website and join our free newsletter to be kept informed and to receive special offers, free chapters, etc.

You can also follow us on Twitter at www.twitter.com/lawbriefpub.

www.ingramcontent.com/pod-product-compliance
Lightning Source LLC
LaVergne TN
LVHW022109200926
848481LV00003B/1126